THE KEY

STUDENT STUDY GUIDE

Social Studies 9

THE KEY student study guide is designed to help students achieve success in school. The content in each study guide is 100% curriculum aligned and serves as an excellent source of material for review and practice. To create this book, teachers, curriculum specialists, and assessment experts have worked closely to develop the instructional pieces that explain each of the key concepts for the course. The practice questions and sample tests have detailed solutions that show problem-solving methods, highlight concepts that are likely to be tested, and point out potential sources of errors. **THE KEY** is a complete guide to be used by students throughout the school year for reviewing and understanding course content, and to prepare for assessments.

Rao, Gautam, 1961 –
THE KEY – Social Studies 9
ISBN: 978-1-77044-430-0

1.   Social Studies – Juvenile Literature. I. Title

Published by
Castle Rock Research Corp.
2000 First & Jasper
10065 Jasper Avenue
Edmonton, AB T5J 3B1

10 9

Publisher
Gautam Rao

Contributors
Brigitta Braden
Heather Friedenthal
Richard Walker

Dedicated to the memory of Dr. V. S. Rao

THE KEY—SOCIAL STUDIES 9

THE KEY consists of the following sections:

KEY Tips for Being Successful at School gives examples of study and review strategies. It includes information about learning styles, study schedules, and note taking for test preparation.

Class Focus includes a unit on each area of the curriculum. Units are divided into sections, each focusing on one of the specific expectations, or main ideas, that students must learn about in that unit. Examples, definitions, and visuals help to explain each main idea. Practice questions on the main ideas are also included. At the end of each unit is a test on the important ideas covered. The practice questions and unit tests help students identify areas they know and those they need to study more. They can also be used as preparation for tests and quizzes. Most questions are of average difficulty, though some are easy and some are hard. Each unit is prefaced by a ***Table of Correlations***, which correlates questions in the unit to the specific curriculum expectations. Answers and solutions are found at the end of each unit.

KEY Strategies for Success on Tests helps students get ready for tests. It shows students different types of questions they might see, word clues to look for when reading them, and hints for answering them.

Practice Tests includes one to three tests based on the entire course. They are very similar to the format and level of difficulty that students may encounter on final tests. In some regions, these tests may be reprinted versions of official tests, or reflect the same difficulty levels and formats as official versions. This gives students the chance to practice using real-world examples. Answers and complete solutions are provided at the end of the section.

For the complete curriculum document (including specific expectations along with examples and sample problems), visit http://education.alberta.ca/teachers/program/socialstudies/programs.aspx.

THE KEY *Study Guides* are available for many courses. Check www.castlerockresearch.com for a complete listing of books available for your area.

For information about any of our resources or services, please call Castle Rock Research at 780.448.9619 or visit our website at http://www.castlerockresearch.com.

At Castle Rock Research, we strive to produce an error-free resource. If you should find an error, please contact us so that future editions can be corrected.

TABLE OF CONTENTS

NOTES

KEY Tips for Being Successful at School

KEY TIPS FOR BEING SUCCESSFUL AT SCHOOL

KEY FACTORS CONTRIBUTING TO SCHOOL SUCCESS

In addition to learning the content of your courses, there are some other things that you can do to help you do your best at school. Some of these strategies are listed below.

- **Keep a positive attitude:** always reflect on what you can already do and what you already know.

- **Be prepared to learn**: have ready the necessary pencils, pens, notebooks, and other required materials for participating in class.

- **Complete all of your assignments:** do your best to finish all of your assignments. Even if you know the material well, practice will reinforce your knowledge. If an assignment or question is difficult for you, work through it as far as you can so that your teacher can see exactly where you are having difficulty.

- **Set small goals for yourself when you are learning new material:** for example, when learning the parts of speech, do not try to learn everything in one night. Work on only one part or section each study session. When you have memorized one particular part of speech and understand it, then move on to another one, continue this process until you have memorized and learned all the parts of speech.

- **Review your classroom work regularly at home:** review to be sure that you understand the material that you learned in class.

- **Ask your teacher for help**: your teacher will help you if you do not understand something or if you are having a difficult time completing your assignments.

- **Get plenty of rest and exercise:** concentrating in class is hard work. It is important to be well-rested and have time to relax and socialize with your friends. This helps you to keep your positive attitude about your school work.

- **Eat healthy meals:** a balanced diet keeps you healthy and gives you the energy that you need for studying at school and at home.

HOW TO FIND YOUR LEARNING STYLE

Every student learns differently. The manner in which you learn best is called your learning style. By knowing your learning style, you can increase your success at school. Most students use a combination of learning styles. Do you know what type of learner you are? Read the following descriptions. Which of these common learning styles do you use most often?

- Linguistic Learner: you may learn best by saying, hearing, and seeing words. You are probably really good at memorizing things such as dates, places, names, and facts. You may need to write and then say out loud the steps in a process, a formula, or the actions that lead up to a significant event.

- Spatial Learner: you may learn best by looking at and working with pictures. You are probably really good at puzzles, imagining things, and reading maps and charts. You may need to use strategies like mind mapping and webbing to organize your information and study notes.

- Kinaesthetic Learner: you may learn best by touching, moving, and figuring things out using manipulative. You are probably really good at physical activities and learning through movement. You may need to draw your finger over a diagram to remember it, "tap out" the steps needed to solve a problem, or "feel" yourself writing or typing a formula.

SCHEDULING STUDY TIME

You should review your class notes regularly to ensure that you have a clear understanding of all the new material you learned. Reviewing your lessons on a regular basis helps you to learn and remember ideas and concepts. It also reduces the quantity of material that you need to study prior to a test. Establishing a study schedule will help you to make the best use of your time.

Regardless of the type of study schedule you use, you may want to consider the following suggestions to maximize your study time and effort:

- Organize your work so that you begin with the most challenging material first.
- Divide the subject's content into small, manageable chunks.
- Alternate regularly between your different subjects and types of study activities in order to maintain your interest and motivation.
- Make a daily list with headings like "Must Do," "Should Do," and "Could Do."
- Begin each study session by quickly reviewing what you studied the day before.
- Maintain your usual routine of eating, sleeping, and exercising to help you concentrate better for extended periods of time.

CREATING STUDY NOTES

MIND-MAPPING OR WEBBING

- Use the key words, ideas, or concepts from your reading or class notes to create a mind map or web (a diagram or visual representation of the given information). A mind map or web is sometimes referred to as a knowledge map.

- Write the key word, concept, theory, or formula in the centre of your page.

- Write down related facts, ideas, events, and information and then link them to the central concept with lines.

- Use coloured markers, underlining, or other symbols to emphasize things such as relationships, time lines, and important information.

- The following mind map is an example of one that could help you develop an essay:

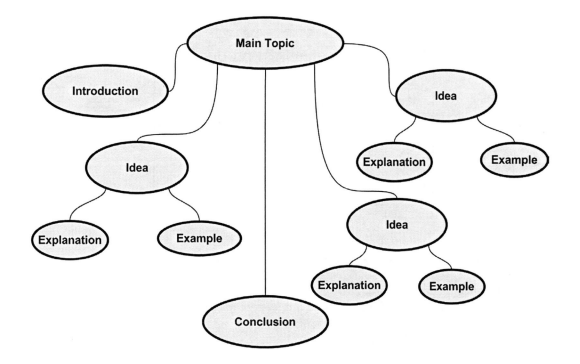

INDEX CARDS

To use index cards while studying, follow these steps:

- Write a key word or question on one side of an index card.
- On the reverse side, write the definition of the word, answer to the question, or any other important information that you want to remember.

```
┌─────────────────────────────────┐
│                                 │
│                                 │
│       What are the means        │
│        of production?           │
│                                 │
│                                 │
└─────────────────────────────────┘
```

```
┌─────────────────────────────────┐
│  What are the means of production? │
│                                 │
│   The means of production are land, │
│        labour and capital       │
│                                 │
└─────────────────────────────────┘
```

SYMBOLS AND STICKY NOTES—IDENTIFYING IMPORTANT INFORMATION

- Use symbols to mark your class notes. For example, an exclamation mark (!) might be used to point out something that must be learned well because it is a very important idea. A question mark (?) may highlight something that you are not certain about, and a diamond (◊) or asterisk (*) could highlight interesting information that you want to remember.
- Use sticky notes when you are not allowed to put marks in books.
- Use sticky notes to mark a page in a book that contains an important diagram, formula, explanation, etc.
- Use sticky notes to mark important facts in research books.

MEMORIZATION TECHNIQUES

- **Association** relates new learning to something you already know. For example, to remember the spelling difference between dessert and desert, recall that the word sand has only one s. So, because there is sand in a desert, the word desert only has on s.

- **Mnemonic** devices are sentences that you create to remember a list or group of items. For example, the first letter of each word in the phrase "**E**very **G**ood **B**oy **D**eserves **F**udge" helps you to remember the names of the lines on the treble clef staff (E, G, B, D, and F) in music.

- **Acronyms** are words that are formed from the first letters or parts of the words in a group. For example, **RADAR** is actually an acronym for **Ra**dio **D**etecting **A**nd **R**anging, and **MASH** is an acronym for **M**obile **A**rmy **S**urgical **H**ospital. **HOMES** helps you to remember the names of the five Great Lakes (**H**uron, **O**ntario, **M**ichigan, **E**rie, and **S**uperior).

- **Visualizing** requires you to use your mind's eye to "see" a chart, list, map, diagram, or sentence as it is in your textbook or notes, on the chalk board or computer screen, or in a display.

- **Initialisms** are abbreviations that are formed from the first letters or parts of the words in a group. Unlike acronyms, initialisms cannot be pronounced as a word themselves. For example, **BEDMAS** is an initialism for the order of operations in math (**B**rackets, **E**xponents, **D**ivide, **M**ultiply, **A**dd, **S**ubtract).

KEY STRATEGIES FOR REVIEWING

Reviewing textbook material, class notes, and handouts should be an ongoing activity. Spending time reviewing becomes more critical when you are preparing for tests. You may find some of the following review strategies useful when studying during your scheduled study time.

- Before reading a selection, preview it by noting the headings, charts, graphs, and chapter questions.
- Read the complete introduction to identify the key information that is addressed in the selection.
- Read the first sentence of the next paragraph for the main idea.
- Skim the paragraph and note the key words, phrases, and information.
- Read the last sentence of the paragraph.
- Repeat this process for each paragraph and section until you have skimmed the entire selection.

KEY STRATEGIES FOR SUCCESS: A CHECKLIST

Review, review, review: review is a huge part of doing well at school and preparing for tests. Here is a checklist for you to keep track of how many suggested strategies for success you are using. Read each question and then put a check mark (✓) in the correct column. Look at the questions where you have checked the "No" column. Think about how you might try using some of these strategies to help you do your best at school.

KEY Strategies for Success	Yes	No
Do you attend school regularly?		
Do you know your personal learning style—how you learn best?		
Do you spend 15 to 30 minutes a day reviewing your notes?		
Do you study in a quiet place at home?		
Do you clearly mark the most important ideas in your study notes?		
Do you use sticky notes to mark texts and research books?		
Do you practise answering multiple-choice and written-response questions?		
Do you ask your teacher for help when you need it?		
Are you maintaining a healthy diet and sleep routine?		
Are you participating in regular physical activity?		

Governance and Rights

GOVERNANCE AND RIGHTS

Table of Correlations				
Specific Expectation	**Practice Questions**	**Unit Test**	**Practice Test 1**	**Practice Test 2**
Students will:				
Demonstrate an understanding and appreciation of how Canada's political processes impact citizenship and identity in an attempt to meet the needs of all Canadians				
9.1.4 examine the structure of Canada's federal political system by exploring and reflecting upon the following questions and issues: • *How are laws passed in the federal political system?* • *What is the relationship between the executive, legislative and judicial branches of Canada's federal political system?* • *What processes are used to determine Members of Parliament and Senators?* • *To whom are Members of Parliament and Senators accountable?* • *What is the role of political parties within Canada's federal political system?* • *What is the role of the media in relation to political issues?* • *How do lobby groups impact government decision making?* • *To what extent do political and legislative processes meet the needs of all Canadians?*	1, 2, 3, 10, 11	1, 2, 14, 15, 16, 17, 18, 19, 20	47, 48, 49	1, 2, 3, 5, 5
9.1.5 analyze the role that citizens and organizations play in Canada's justice system by exploring and reflecting upon the following questions and issues: • *How do citizens and organizations participate in Canada's justice system?* • *What are citizens' legal roles and their responsibilities?* • *What is the intention of the Youth Criminal Justice Act?*	4, 5, 6, 12, 13	3, 4, 5, 6, 9, 10	1, 2, 3, 4, 50	6, 7
9.1.6 assess, critically, the impact of the Canadian Charter of Rights and Freedoms on the legislative process in Canada by exploring and reflecting upon the following questions and issues: • *In what ways has the Canadian Charter of Rights and Freedoms fostered recognition of individual rights in Canada?* • *How does the Canadian Charter of Rights and Freedoms support individuals in exercising their rights?* • *In what ways has the Canadian Charter of Rights and Freedoms affected conditions in the workplace?* • *What is the relationship between the rights guaranteed in the Canadian Charter of Rights and Freedoms and the responsibilities of Canadian citizens?*	7	7, 8, 21	5, 6, 7, 8, 29, 30, 31, 41	8, 9, 10, 11, 12, 13, 14

| 9.1.7 | assess, critically, how the increased demand for recognition of collective rights has impacted the legislative process in Canada by exploring and reflecting upon the following questions and issues:

• In what ways has the Canadian Charter of Rights and Freedoms fostered recognition of collective rights in Canada?
• In what ways does the Canadian Charter of Rights and Freedoms meet the needs of Francophones in minority settings?
• To what extend does the Canadian Charter of Rights and Freedoms meet the needs of Francophones in Quebec?
• To what extent should federal and provincial governments support and promote the rights of official language minorities in Canada?
• How does the Indian Act recognize the status and identity of Aboriginal peoples?
• How does legislation such as Treaty 6, Treaty 7 and Treaty 8 recognize the status and identity of Aboriginal peoples?
• How do governments recognize Métis cultures and rights through legislation? | 8, 9, 14, 15 | 11, 12, 22, 23 | 9, 10, 11, 12, 42 | 15, 16 |
| 9.1.8 | assess, critically, how legislative processes attempt to address emerging issues of immigration by exploring and reflecting upon the following questions and issues"

• What factors influence immigration policies in Canada?
• How are changes to Canadian policies on immigration and refugees a reflection of world issues?
• What impact does increasing immigration have on Aboriginal peoples and communities?
• How are provincial governments able to influence and implement immigration policies?
• How is the implementation of immigration policies in Quebec an attempt to strengthen the French language in North America?
• What is the relationship between immigration policies in Canada and the rights guaranteed in the Canadian Charter of Rights and Freedoms?
• To what extent does Canada benefit from immigration? | 16, 17, 18 | 13, 24, 25, 26 | 13, 14, 15, 16, 17, 32, 33, 34, 43, 44, 45, 46 | 17, 18, 19, 20, 21, 33, 34 |

ISSUES FOR CANADIANS: GOVERNANCE AND RIGHTS

9.1.4   examine the structure of Canada's federal political system by exploring and reflecting upon the following questions and issues

THE STRUCTURE OF CANADA'S FEDERAL POLITICAL SYSTEM

WHAT IS THE RELATIONSHIP BETWEEN THE EXECUTIVE, LEGISLATIVE, AND JUDICIAL BRANCHES OF CANADA'S FEDERAL POLITICAL SYSTEM?

Canada's federal government is made up of three branches, each with distinct roles and responsibilities. The **legislative branch** consists of the House of Commons (all elected members of Parliament), the Senate (appointed by the prime minister), and the Governor General (the Queen's representative in Canada). More commonly, the legislative branch is referred to as Parliament. The duty of the legislative branch is to propose, amend, and pass laws in Canada. Because all elected members of Parliament are members of the legislative branch, there are various political parties represented within it.

The **executive branch** consists of the prime minister, the cabinet, and the public service, and its role is to carry out the laws passed by the legislative branch of the government. The cabinet is a group of members of Parliament appointed by the prime minister to be responsible for specific areas important to Canadians. These areas are called portfolios, and the member of Parliament in charge of them is called a minister. Some examples of portfolios are health, defence, finance, and the environment. The public service consists of people employed by the government who are not elected and whose jobs generally do not change as a result of an election. Elected members of the executive branch represent the same political party—whichever party forms the government. The executive branch is responsible for the daily duties of running the country and serving the interests of Canadians.

The **judicial branch** consists of Canada's courts, including the superior provincial courts, the court of appeal, the Supreme Court, as well as other federal courts. This branch of the government is kept completely separate from the other branches in order to provide a check of powers on the executive and legislative branches. The judicial branch interprets laws made by the legislative branch to ensure the rights of Canadians are protected.

HOW ARE LAWS PASSED IN THE FEDERAL POLITICAL SYSTEM?

In Canada, laws are passed by the legislative branch of the government, which includes the House of Commons, the Senate, and the Governor General. Before an idea can be made into a law, it must first be presented as a bill to the House of Commons. Here, it goes through a first reading, during which there is no debate or changes made. Next, the bill enters the second reading, during which the ideas behind the bill and its merits for Canadians are debated. During the second reading, there is a vote on the bill, and it will either pass to the committee stage or be rejected. At the committee stage, a small group of members of Parliament work with citizens and other stakeholders or experts to decide if the bill should be amended (changed) in any way. The group usually makes a recommendation as to whether the bill should be accepted or rejected. The bill is then presented to the House of Commons again, and members debate and vote on the proposed changes. The last phase is the third reading, during which members in the House of Commons vote on the finalized bill.

Next, the bill must go through a similar process in the Senate. The Senate may recommend more amendments to the bill, which the House of Commons will again debate and either accept or reject. Although the Senate has the power to block a bill from becoming law, it rarely uses this power. The main role of the Senate is to provide a second thought to potential laws.

After the bill has passed through the House of Commons and the Senate, it must be given royal assent by the Governor General. Because the role of the Governor General is largely symbolic, royal assent is always given, although technically the Governor General does have the power to block a bill from becoming law.

WHAT PROCESSES ARE USED TO DETERMINE THE MEMBERS OF PARLIAMENT AND SENATORS?

Members of Parliament (MPs) hold seats in the House of Commons and are elected by the citizens of Canada through a process called "representation by population." They are the representatives of the Canadian citizens. Canada is divided into areas called ridings (or constituencies) based on how many people live in an area. Some ridings, such as those in northern areas of Canada, are geographically much larger than those in urban areas because the population density is much less in northern areas than it is in a city. During an election, citizens in each riding are able to vote for the candidate they would like to represent them in the government. Each party may have one candidate run in each riding. The candidate who wins the most votes in each riding wins a seat in the House of Commons, and the party that wins the most seats forms the government.

Senators are appointed by the prime minister. Senators represent a variety of political parties and may retain their posts until the age of 75.

The term Parliament encompasses each of the following groups: the House of Commons, the Senate, and the monarch.

TO WHOM ARE MEMBERS OF PARLIAMENT AND SENATORS ACCOUNTABLE?

Members of Parliament and senators are accountable to the citizens of Canada and should consider the best interests of Canadians at all times. Specifically, members of Parliament are accountable to the people who elected them in their constituency—they are the voice of those citizens in Parliament. Senators have a particular responsibility to minorities in Canada—to make sure that the issues and concerns of minorities are addressed in Parliament.

WHAT IS THE ROLE OF POLITICAL PARTIES IN CANADA'S FEDERAL POLITICAL SYSTEM?

Political parties are organizations of people with similar values and ideas about the best way to govern Canada. The way the government makes decisions is largely based on these values and differs greatly from party to party. These ideas and values are referred to as a party's platform. Citizens can examine these platforms and decide which party best relates to their own values and beliefs. During an election, members of each party campaign to win support through votes. The party that wins the most seats forms the government. Although the majority of elected members of Parliament and people who run in elections represent a political party, people can run and be elected as an independent—someone who does not represent a political party.

WHAT IS THE ROLE OF THE MEDIA IN RELATION TO POLITICAL ISSUES?

The term media refers to the Internet, newspapers, television, radio, advertising, and magazines. In relation to political issues, the media functions to inform citizens about government ideas, actions, and decisions. However, the media is also very powerful and adept at influencing citizens' perspectives and beliefs about government or politics. The media may put a "spin" on the way a particular issue is reported, which can influence how it is perceived by its audience. Politicians carefully choose their words when dealing with the media, as they are aware that the media can have a very positive or very negative influence on their political careers. Sometimes the media exposes scandals or information, which reveals corruption in the government about which citizens otherwise may not have been made aware. Other times, it can be very difficult for citizens to get the whole story from the media.

HOW DO LOBBY GROUPS IMPACT GOVERNMENT DECISION-MAKING?

Lobby groups are organizations that work to influence government decisions about specific issues. Lobby groups hire people (lobbyists) to bring their issue to the forefront of the minds of Canadians, and they put pressure on the government to make policies that support their issue. Lobby groups also use the media to influence public views about their issues and try to have the general population put pressure on the government to implement changes or introduce policies to support their goals. For example, Mothers Against Drunk Driving (MADD) is a lobby group that works to change government policies to increase the severity of punishments given to people convicted of impaired driving. The group also works to publicize the dangers of impaired driving and to change public perception about the acceptability of this practice.

TO WHAT EXTENT DO POLITICAL AND LEGISLATIVE PROCESSES MEET THE NEEDS OF ALL CANADIANS?

The extent to which the needs of all Canadians are met by Canada's political and legislative process varies with each Canadian. For those who are able to be actively involved in the process or have the means to have their opinions and concerns heard, their needs are more easily addressed. Some Canadians feel that their issues and concerns are not the priority of the government, while others do not have the means to become involved in the process; often, these people feel alienated.

9.1.5   analyze the role that citizens and organizations play in Canada's justice system by exploring and reflecting upon the following questions and issues

THE ROLE OF CITIZENS AND ORGANIZATIONS IN CANADA'S JUSTICE SYSTEM

HOW DO CITIZENS AND ORGANIZATIONS PARTICIPATE IN CANADA'S JUSTICE SYSTEM?

Canadians can participate in the justice system in many ways. One of these is by serving jury duty. Citizens are randomly selected for jury duty, and it is considered to be a responsibility of Canadian citizens to fulfill this duty. People can be exempted from jury duty if they can prove it will cause them undue hardship. Employers must allow employees time off if they are summoned, but they do not have to pay them for the time missed from work.

Knowing the law is another way in which citizens can participate in Canada's justice system, as citizens are then aware of their rights and what is permitted in Canadian society. Claiming ignorance about a law someone may be accused of breaking is not considered a defence in Canada.

Advocacy (working on behalf of an idea, policy, or person) is another way in which people can be involved in the justice system. Citizens may advocate for an issue they feel strongly about through a lobby group or their own means of communication with the government, such as contacting their member of Parliament. The John Howard Society is an organization that is separate from government. This society works to find out why youths and adults commit crimes, and the organization tries to find solutions to prevent crime. The society works with people who have committed crimes and tries to ensure their rights are being respected. They also work to help those who have been released from prison to integrate successfully back into society. The Elizabeth Fry Society is a similar organization that advocates on behalf of women and girls who have been accused of or convicted of crimes. The society attempts to find the root causes for female criminal activity and bring those issues into the public eye. As with the John Howard Society, this society also helps women and girls integrate successfully back into society after serving their punishment and helps prevent them from committing a crime again.

WHAT ARE CITIZENS' LEGAL ROLES AND RESPONSIBILITIES?

In exchange for the rights provided to citizens in Canada, citizens have certain responsibilities and legal roles they should fulfill. These include participation in the democratic process through voting, becoming informed about government actions, and communicating with their elected representatives. Citizens are also responsible for knowing Canadian laws and abiding by them.

WHAT IS THE INTENTION OF THE YOUTH CRIMINAL JUSTICE ACT?

The Youth Criminal Justice Act (YCJA) replaced the former legislation dealing with youth crime, the Young Offenders Act, in 2003. Generally, the YCJA focuses on the rehabilitation of young criminals but also carries heavier punishment for youth convicted of serious and violent crimes. The YCJA aims to help young people who get in trouble with the law to understand how their actions affect other people and to deter them from committing crimes again.

9.1.6   assess, critically, the impact of the Canadian Charter of Rights and Freedoms on the legislative process in Canada by exploring and reflecting upon the following questions and issues

THE IMPACT OF THE CANADIAN CHARTER OF RIGHTS AND FREEDOMS ON THE LEGISLATIVE PROCESS

IN WHAT WAYS HAS THE CANADIAN CHARTER OF RIGHTS AND FREEDOMS FOSTERED RECOGNITION OF INDIVIDUAL RIGHTS IN CANADA?

When the Charter of Rights and Freedoms was entrenched in the Canadian Constitution in 1982, the rights of Canadians and people living in Canada were made universal across the country. Because they are part of the Constitution, these rights must be considered when all other laws are being written and passed in Canada. The rights of the individual also became more widely recognized with the introduction of the charter, as these rights are stated explicitly within the charter, and with the exception of two rights (voting and moving in or out of the country), they are applicable to all people living in Canada.

How Does the Canadian Charter of Rights and Freedoms Support Individuals in Exercising Their Rights?

According to the charter, individuals have certain rights and fundamental freedoms that can only be restricted if the act of an individual exercising his or her rights infringes on the rights of another individual. Some of the individual rights listed in the charter include the right to freedom of expression and peaceful association with any group. There are also rights that relate to an individual's relationship with the government and legal system, such as the right to vote (for citizens only) and the right to a fair and expedient trial. All people also have the right not to be discriminated against because of race, ethnicity, religion, gender, or disability. In addition, although it is not specifically listed in the charter, sexual orientation has been read in by the Supreme Court of Canada as another reason for which people may not be discriminated against. If an individual feels that his or her rights have been restricted, that person can lodge a complaint with an organization such as the Human Rights Commission. In some cases, these complaints may be taken to court, and in even fewer cases, the court decision may result in a change to a law.

In What Ways Has the Canadian Charter of Rights and Freedoms Affected Conditions In the Workplace?

Since the introduction of the charter, employers have been made more aware of discrimination in their place of business. Employers must ensure that all employees are being treated in accordance with the charter. For example, gender issues have arisen in which women have successfully demanded to be paid equally for doing the same work as men. Workplaces must be careful not to discriminate against an employee based on his or her age, race, or religion. For example, the Royal Canadian Mounted Police has made allowances for Sikh officers to wear specially designed turbans rather than the traditional RCMP headgear. In addition, an employer may not fire someone based on his or her age. A person has the right not to be fired for taking time off for a religious holiday, even when it is not observed by the rest of the company or organization.

What is the Relationship Between the Rights Guaranteed in the Canadian Charter of Rights and Freedoms and The Responsibilities of Canadian Citizens?

In exchange for the rights provided for individuals in the charter, the government asks for individuals to fulfill certain responsibilities. These include involvement in the political process, social responsibilities, and paying taxes, among others. Although these responsibilities are expected of individuals in Canada, an individual will not be excluded from the rights included in the charter if she or he does not fulfill them. However, a person may face punishment for neglecting certain responsibilities, such as paying taxes.

9.1.7 assess, critically, how the increased demand for recognition of collective rights has impacted the legislative process in Canada by exploring and reflecting upon the following questions and issues

THE IMPACT OF THE RECOGNITION OF COLLECTIVE RIGHTS

IN WHAT WAYS HAS THE CANADIAN CHARTER OF RIGHTS AND FREEDOMS FOSTERED RECOGNITION OF COLLECTIVE RIGHTS IN CANADA?

Collective rights are rights awarded to a specific group of people. In the Charter of Rights and Freedoms, the collective rights of Francophones and Anglophones in Canada are specifically laid out. In Section 35 of the Constitution, the collective rights of Aboriginal peoples in Canada are described. By including collective rights in the Constitution and the Charter of Rights and Freedoms, these groups are more easily able to ensure that their cultures and languages are protected.

IN WHAT WAYS DOES THE CANADIAN CHARTER OF RIGHTS AND FREEDOMS MEET THE NEEDS OF FRANCOPHONES IN MINORITY SETTINGS?

When someone is in a minority setting, such as a Francophone living in a primarily English-speaking community, it can be difficult to maintain that minority culture and language. The charter guarantees that no matter where a Francophone person lives, that person has the right to access government services in French and, when there are enough students to warrant it, access to publicly funded education in French.

TO WHAT EXTENT DOES THE CANADIAN CHARTER OF RIGHTS AND FREEDOMS MEET THE NEEDS OF FRANCOPHONES IN QUEBEC?

Under the charter, French is named as one of the two official languages of Canada. In the province of Quebec, the official language is French. The charter helps to promote the French culture in Quebec by ensuring that the rights of Francophones are protected; for example, the right to access government services in French and the right to educate the province's Francophone children in French. However, it also limits the use of French as the only language in the province. For example, businesses in Quebec are allowed to display any language as long as French is also displayed.

TO WHAT EXTENT SHOULD FEDERAL AND PROVINCIAL GOVERNMENTS SUPPORT AND PROMOTE THE LANGUAGE RIGHTS OF MINORITIES IN CANADA?

The Canadian government has a responsibility to protect the rights of all minorities (including minority language rights) in Canada. Canada prides itself on having a multicultural identity and on being a country that has great respect for human rights. The Canadian government has a responsibility to make sure that these cultures are protected. The government should ensure that legislation is in place that not only promotes language minorities but ensures that they are able to flourish.

How Does The Indian Act Recognize The Status And Identity Of Aboriginal Peoples?

The Indian Act is a law that was first passed in 1876. Its purpose was to allow the government to administer the rights guaranteed to First Nations people in the "numbered treaties." When it was first written, the act also had the purpose of assimilating First Nations people into mainstream Canadian culture by imposing rules of governance on them and attempting to extinguish First Nations culture. The act defines who is a "status Indian" and therefore entitled to the rights associated with that title. Many First Nations people feel the act is still discriminatory and inhibits First Nation identity, as it does not allow for self-governance and the recognition of nationhood among First Nations groups. The act has been amended various times, and there have been attempts to replace it with another law, which so far have not been successful.

How Does Legislation, Such As Treaty 6, Treaty 7, And Treaty 8, Recognize the Status and Identity of Aboriginal Peoples?

Treaties 6, 7, and 8 are three of the 11 treaties that were signed by First Nations groups and Great Britain and Canada between 1871 and 1921. The treaties were agreements between the groups over land and compensation for that land. In the treaties, First Nations people agreed to share the land in exchange for guarantees from the Canadian government, such as protection of land, resource usage, and the provision of education, health, and other issues. First Nations people view the treaties as permanent and believe that they did not give up their land, but rather agreed to live in harmony with the Europeans on that land. However, the Canadian government disagrees, and as a result, there have been many conflicts between the government and the First Nations people over land claims in the treaties. In addition, the First Nations' records of the treaties, which were both oral and written, contradict the written records of the government, causing further disagreements. First Nations people see the treaties as the way to maintain their culture and identity, as the treaties provided certain guarantees that the First Nations' way of life (such as hunting, fishing, trapping, and their relationship with the land) would not be compromised.

How Do Governments Recognize Métis Cultures And Rights Through Legislation?

Métis culture in Canada is distinct from the other two Aboriginal groups in Canada (First Nations and Inuit), and as a result, governments have worked to find unique legislation to recognize Métis culture and rights. Although the Métis were not part of the numbered treaties signed by the First Nations people, the Métis have made other treaties (agreements) with the government. For example, the Manitoba Act is considered by many Métis people to be a treaty between them and the Canadian government. Louis Riel was instrumental in the creation of the act, which recognized Manitoba as a province. As a result of the act, land was granted to the Métis people. However, as a result of the conflict that followed, many Métis either fled Manitoba or never received the land that was promised to them. In an effort to address issues surrounding land claims and governance, the Alberta-Métis Settlement Accord (a collection of legislation aimed to provide autonomy and economic self-sufficiency for the Métis) was proclaimed in 1990. There are eight Métis settlements in Alberta, which together cover 528 000 hectares of land and have a collective population of approximately 8 000. Each settlement is governed by a council, which has the ability to pass bylaws and make decisions for the settlement as long as any bylaws and decisions do not contradict provincial or federal law. The councils govern the day-to-day lives of the Métis people living on the settlements. There is a larger organization—the Métis Settlements General Council—that works to advocate for the issues of the settlements as a collective and makes some regulations that are binding on all the settlements. The Métis settlements in Alberta are the only ones of their kind in Canada.

9.1.8   assess, critically, how legislative processes attempt to address emerging issues of immigration by exploring and reflecting upon the following questions and issues

EMERGING ISSUES OF IMMIGRATION

WHAT FACTORS INFLUENCE IMMIGRATION POLICIES IN CANADA?

Immigration is when people leave their homes to go and live in another country. Canada is a country in which many people want to live. The Canadian government must make sure that the people who come here will be good for Canada and the people already living here. In order to do this, the government makes policies about who is or is not allowed to come to live in Canada.

Several factors influence the government's decision about who is allowed to come to Canada. The first of these is economic. People who have skills and knowledge that would benefit Canada's economy are considered desirable, as are those people who have already been offered jobs in Canada, because they will contribute to the economy almost immediately from the time they arrive. However, the government also knows that population growth can help boost the economy, so having more people living here can be beneficial. Canada accepts more of this type of immigrant than any other.

Another factor is politics. In some countries, people are persecuted as a result of their political or religious beliefs. These people can apply to come to Canada under refugee status. Accepting these immigrants can make a political statement that Canada does not condone such persecution by other governments and can affirm Canada's commitment to human rights. Other people may be forced to leave their homes because of war or other violence, and these people may also apply to come to Canada under refugee status.

The health of potential immigrants is another factor the Canadian government considers when reviewing applications for immigration. With the exception of those immigrating under refugee or family status, a person may be refused entry if she or he has a dangerous contagious disease or one that would put a large strain on Canada's health system, such as AIDS. Some mental conditions may also be reason for the government to restrict a person's entry to Canada.

Security of the nation and the people living here is another factor that the Canadian government considers carefully when drafting immigration policies and laws. The government does not want to admit anyone to Canada who has engaged in activity deemed by the Canadian government to be subversive or who is a member of a group that has engaged in such activities.

HOW ARE CHANGES TO CANADIAN POLICIES ON IMMIGRATION AND REFUGEES A REFLECTION OF WORLD ISSUES?

Canada's immigration policies have changed dramatically since Confederation. World events and issues have had a major effect on the decisions made by Canada's government about who is allowed to come to Canada. For example, largely because of the events of and following September 11, 2001, Canada's immigration laws changed quite significantly in an attempt to prevent those involved in terrorist activities from entering Canada. Global standards and domestic policies for human rights have also influenced changes in Canada's immigration policies over many decades. At various times throughout history, people were denied entry to Canada or laws were written in such a way that made it impossible for people to come to Canada because of their ethnicity or race. Under today's laws and according to the Charter of Rights and Freedoms, such qualifiers are no longer reason enough to deny the entry of an applicant for immigration to Canada.

WHAT IMPACT DOES INCREASING IMMIGRATION HAVE ON ABORIGINAL PEOPLES AND COMMUNITIES?

From the perspective of many Aboriginal people and leaders in Canada, the Canadian government does not adequately address the needs and issues facing Aboriginal peoples. As a result, immigration is believed to further compound these issues, as the government seeks foreigners to fill jobs that could be filled by Aboriginal people if issues believed to be barriers for Aboriginals to access education and training were addressed.

HOW ARE PROVINCIAL GOVERNMENTS ABLE TO INFLUENCE AND IMPLEMENT IMMIGRATION POLICIES?

Because the populations and economies of Canada's provinces vary so greatly, their need and desire for immigrants also varies. For example, Alberta's economy is one of the fastest growing in Canada and has been experiencing an economic boom and labour shortage for several years. The need for workers, specifically workers knowledgeable or skilled in areas such as oil and gas, is very high, whereas in other provinces, such a need does not exist. Many different areas of Alberta's economy report that they do not have enough workers to meet their business potential. Although the provinces cannot make decisions about who is allowed to immigrate, the Provincial Nomination Program allows provinces to specify the need for immigrants in particular areas as well as to set up recruitment in other countries.

HOW IS THE IMPLEMENTATION OF IMMIGRATION POLICIES IN QUEBEC AN ATTEMPT TO STRENGTHEN THE FRENCH LANGUAGE IN NORTH AMERICA?

In an effort to preserve the Francophone culture in Quebec and North America, the Canada-Quebec Accord was signed in 1991. This allows Quebec to choose French-speaking immigrants from around the world, although the federal government officially clears these people for immigration to Canada. In addition, the accord allows Quebec to insist that immigrants send their children to French schools or enroll in French programs. This policy has increased the number of French-speaking immigrants coming to Canada, and as a result has helped to preserve and promote the Francophone culture in Quebec and in turn, North America.

WHAT IS THE RELATIONSHIP BETWEEN IMMIGRATION POLICIES IN CANADA AND THE RIGHTS GUARANTEED IN THE CANADIAN CHARTER OF RIGHTS AND FREEDOMS?

Since the implementation of the charter, people seeking immigration to Canada have more rights than they did previous to 1982. Because the Supreme Court stated that the rights guaranteed in the charter apply to all people physically in Canada, any immigrant who has made it to Canadian soil is protected by the charter. As a result, if a potential immigrant's application is denied, they have the right to a hearing and to remain in Canada until their trial. In addition, for those seeking immigration under refugee status, the government will provide them with necessities until a decision is made about their application.

TO WHAT EXTENT DOES CANADA BENEFIT FROM IMMIGRATION?

There are many ways in which Canada benefits from immigration, although this is a matter of perspective. Examples of benefits to Canada might include a stronger economy as a result of more workers for companies and a larger market. In addition, a major part of Canada's identity is its multicultural makeup, so the arrival of many people from places all around the world helps to solidify this part of Canada's identity. The perception of Canada on the world stage as a welcoming country with a thriving economy is also good for Canada's role in world politics and economics.

PRACTICE QUESTIONS—GOVERNANCE AND RIGHTS

1. Canada's Parliament is made up of
   A. members of Parliament
   B. members of Parliament and senators
   C. the monarch, the Senate, and the House of Commons
   D. the monarch, the Senate, the House of Commons, and the Supreme Court

Use the following information to answer the next two questions.

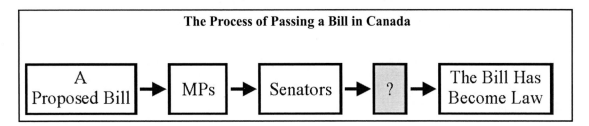

2. The given diagram can be correctly completed by replacing the question mark with the term
   A. caucus members
   B. cabinet ministers
   C. the prime minister
   D. the Governor General

3. In the given diagram, which stage of the bill-passing process is indicated by the question mark?
   A. Royal assent
   B. Third reading
   C. The report stage
   D. The committee stage

4. Each of the following scenarios is an example of a failure to live up to one's responsibilities as a citizen **except**
   A. quitting a political party
   B. cheating on an income tax form
   C. lying to a judge to get out of jury duty
   D. neglecting to exercise the right to vote

5. The principle of responsible citizenship encourages citizens to

   A. become apathetic about national problems

   B. give more unconditional obedience to political leaders

   C. rely less on the government for the betterment of society

   D. concern themselves more with their rights as a citizen than with their citizenship duties

6. Which of the following goals is **not** part of the Youth Criminal Justice Act?

   A. Removing the distinction between a youth and an adult when dealing with serious and violent crimes

   B. Rehabilitating young people so they no longer participate in criminal activity

   C. Using punishment as a consequence for youths involved in criminal activity

   D. Helping young people reintegrate into society after committing a crime

7. The process of the strengthening of a right by specifically mentioning it in the Constitution is called

   A. rightism

   B. patriation

   C. entrenchment

   D. constitutionalism

8. Along with the Canadian government (represented by the Queen), which of the following groups of people are represented by Treaties 6, 7, and 8?

   A. First Nations

   B. Aboriginals

   C. Métis

   D. Inuit

9. Which of the following statements about the Métis settlements is **false**?

   A. The rules governing the Métis settlements are similar to those governing the First Nations reserves.

   B. Councils on the Métis settlements have the ability to make bylaws that apply only to the settlements.

   C. A form of self-governance exists on the Métis settlements.

   D. The Métis settlements exist only in Alberta.

10. The **primary** role of the executive branch of the government is to

    A. make laws

    B. enforce laws

    C. set punishments for lawbreakers

    D. determine if laws have been broken

11. Which electoral system is used to select Canada's members of Parliament?

    A. Canvassing

    B. Popular vote

    C. First past the post

    D. Proportional representation

12. Which of the following generalizations about the Youth Criminal Justice Act (YCJA) is **most** accurate?

    A. The YCJA seeks to find harsh punishments for youths who commit crimes in order to deter them from becoming serious criminals as adults.

    B. According to the spirit of the YCJA, society as a whole will benefit more from individualized treatment of young offenders than a catch-all piece of legislation.

    C. Because society has a low tolerance for criminals, the spirit of the YCJA is to impress this on young people through tough penalties for all crimes committed by youths.

    D. Under the YCJA, youths are treated as adults as much as possible in order to teach them that committing crimes is very serious and can result in very undesirable punishments.

13. Which of the following characteristics describes a role fulfilled by the John Howard and Elizabeth Fry societies?

    A. Advocating on the behalf of criminals

    B. Crafting legislation to deal with serious crime

    C. Providing support for victims of violent crime

    D. Deciding on punishments for young offenders

14. Which of the following statements about the Indian Act is **false**?

    A. The act guarantees the land claims described in the numbered treaties.

    B. The original act attempted to assimilate First Nations people.

    C. The act is today considered by some to be discriminatory.

    D. The act defines who is a status Indian in Canada.

15. Which of the following groupings of legislation set out the terms for the First Nations reserves in Canada?

    A. Alberta-Métis Settlements Accord

    B. Canadian Constitution

    C. Numbered treaties

    D. Indian Act

16. Which of the following scenarios is an example of Canada using immigration as a means of expressing its views on human rights?

    A. Allowing the immigration of a woman from Germany with skills in the computer programming industry

    B. Preventing the immigration of a man who has served time in jail for theft in South Africa

    C. Allowing the immigration of a man who practises a religion that is illegal in Cuba

    D. Preventing the immigration of a woman with ties to a terrorist organization in Syria

17. Although Canada's immigration laws state that a person may be denied entry to the country if their health poses too much of a burden for the health system, which of the following potential immigrants may be exempted from this rule?

    A. A woman from Sudan fleeing a civil war

    B. A man from China who works as a courier

    C. A doctor from France with no family in Canada

    D. An engineer from Mexico who has a job arranged in Toronto

18. In 2005, which of the following groups of Canadians called on the Canadian government to freeze immigration to Canada until issues in its community were addressed?

    A. Anglophones

    B. First Nations

    C. Francophones

    D. New Canadians

24

ANSWERS AND SOLUTIONS—PRACTICE QUESTIONS

1. C	5. C	9. A	13. A	17. A
2. D	6. A	10. B	14. A	18. B
3. A	7. C	11. C	15. C	
4. A	8. A	12. B	16. C	

1. C

Canada's Parliament is made up of the monarch (or his or her representative, the Governor General), the Senate, and the House of Commons. Parliament is the legislative (lawmaking) branch of Canada's government; all three parts of Parliament play a role in the making of Canada's laws.

Canada's Parliament is made up of three parts—not merely one or two. Furthermore, it does not include the Supreme Court of Canada. Parliament is a legislative body; the Supreme Court is a judicial body.

2. D

The final step in the legislative process is royal assent. This formal approval is given by the Governor General (or, on rare occasions, by the monarch, who the Governor General represents). No Canadian bill can become a law without having been given royal assent.

A caucus (members of Parliament who belong to a particular political party), cabinet ministers, and the prime minister do not participate in the final step of the bill-passing process.

3. A

The final stage in the bill-passing process is called royal assent. In this stage, the Governor General (or the monarch) signs the bill into law.

The third reading is the final step in the bill-passing process in the House of Commons and in the Senate—but not the final step in the overall legislative process. The report stage and the committee stage take place in the House of Commons before the third reading of a bill.

4. A

Quitting a political party is not an example of irresponsible citizenship. Sometimes a person may decide to do this because he or she feels that the party is not serving the best interests of the nation. Quitting for this reason could be the responsible thing for a citizen to do.

All of these actions (cheating on an income tax return, neglecting to vote, and lying to a judge to get out of jury duty) are examples of irresponsible citizenship.

5. C

The principle of responsible citizenship encourages each citizen to take personal responsibility for the welfare of the country. In other words, it encourages a citizen to rely less on the government for the benefit of society.

Responsible citizenship is opposed to apathy (indifference) to national problems.
It rejects blind obedience to political leaders, and it holds that citizenship responsibilities are just as important as the rights of citizenship.

6. A

The Youth Criminal Justice Act clearly states that young people should not be treated the same as adults and that their level of maturity must be considered when deciding on a consequence for criminal activity.

Rehabilitation, consequence, and reintegration are all aspects of the Youth Criminal Justice Act that are used as retribution and deterrence of future criminal activity for youths who have committed crimes.

7. C

The process of strengthening a right by specifically mentioning it in the Constitution is known as entrenchment. All of the rights listed in Canada's Charter of Rights and Freedoms are entrenched rights.

Rightism is the favouring of right-wing (conservative) political and economic policies. Patriation refers to the process of gaining complete national control over something that was previously (completely or partly) controlled by a foreign government. Constitutionalism is the belief in a constitutional system of government (a political system in which the rules of the Constitution are respected).

8. A

Treaties 6, 7, and 8 were agreements between the Canadian government and the First Nations peoples.

Neither the Inuit nor the Métis were part of those treaties. As the term *Aboriginal* refers to all three groups, it is also incorrect.

9. A

The Métis settlements are not regulated by the federal government and do not operate similarly to the First Nations reserves.

The other three statements about the Métis settlements are correct.

10. B

The executive branch of the government enforces laws.

The legislative branch makes laws.
The judicial branch determines if laws have been broken and sets punishments for lawbreakers.

11. C

"First past the post" refers to the number of votes a candidate receives in a riding or electoral district. The candidate with the most votes in a riding wins a seat in the House of Commons.

Canvassing is the process of visiting homes during an election campaign in the attempt to win over voters. The term *popular vote* refers to the percentage of the total votes that a party received in an election. Proportional representation is an electoral system used in many European countries whereby seats in the legislature are awarded to parties on the basis of the popular vote; for example, in a proportional representation system, a party that receives 25% of the popular vote would receive approximately 25% of the seats in the legislative assembly.

12. B

When it was written, the YCJA aimed to treat young offenders on an individual basis, taking into account various factors when dictating punishments for crimes. Although youths can face very serious punishments, the act intends to rehabilitate youths in order to prevent them from becoming criminals as adults.

None of the other descriptions of the YCJA are accurate.

13. A

Both the John Howard and Elizabeth Fry societies work with those accused and convicted of crimes to ensure their rights are being protected. These societies also help people re-integrate into society after serving their punishments, among other things.

Neither society decides on punishments, crafts legislation, or works with victims of crime.

14. A

The Indian Act was a way for the government to administer the terms of the numbered treaties but did not prescribe any land guarantees to First Nations peoples.

Each of the other statements about the act is true.

15. C

Under the numbered treaties, the First Nations people and the Canadian government made agreements about land and services. In addition, they set out the framework for the reserve system in Canada.

None of the other groupings of legislation established the reserve system.

16. C

According to the Charter of Rights and Freedoms in Canada, practising one's religion is a fundamental freedom. By allowing someone to immigrate who is legally not allowed to practise his or her religion in his or her home country, Canada is demonstrating its disagreement with such a policy.

Accepting someone with computer programming skills is potentially beneficial to Canada's economy and not a statement on human rights. Preventing the immigration of someone connected to a terrorist organization or who has been convicted of a crime deemed reasonable by Canadian standards is not a statement on human rights but rather a way of protecting Canadian society from potentially dangerous people.

17. A

The regulations about the health of potential immigrants do not apply to people who are trying to immigrate to Canada under refugee or family-class status.

None of the other potential immigrants would be attempting to immigrate under those circumstances and so would not be exempted.

18. B

In 2005, the Assembly of First Nations called on the Canadian government to freeze immigration until the conditions of many First Nations people in Canada were improved. Some First Nations believe that the government should work harder to ensure that all First Nations people have access to education, training, and support, which would allow them to fill the jobs the government sometimes seeks to fill through immigration.

UNIT TEST—GOVERNANCE AND RIGHTS

1. Who decides what bills will be introduced to Canada's Parliament?

    A. The whip

    B. The Governor General

    C. The prime minister and the cabinet

    D. The Speaker in the House of Commons

2. The **greatest** number of Canadians actively participate in which of the following activities?

    A. Voting

    B. Joining a political party

    C. Running as a candidate in an election

    D. Assisting a candidate with a political campaign

3. Which of the following assemblies uses the principle of regional representation—not representation by population—to determine its membership?

    A. Canada's Senate

    B. Quebec's national assembly

    C. Canada's House of Commons

    D. Alberta's legislative assembly

Use the following source to answer the next question.

Rights in Canada
I Right to vote by secret ballot in an election
II Right to free speech
III Right to freedom of assembly
IV Right to fair trial
V Right to worship as you choose

4. Which of the given rights would be considered a political right?

    A. I

    B. II

    C. IV

    D. V

5. One responsibility of the legislative branch of government in Canada is to
   A. carry out decisions made by the government
   B. decide how criminals will be punished
   C. decide who has broken the law
   D. pass laws for the country

6. One example of the political responsibilities held by Canadian citizens is
   A. voting
   B. serving jury duty
   C. respecting the rights of others
   D. participating in the community

7. One example of the way in which the Canadian Charter of Rights and Freedoms protects Francophones when they are the minority in an area is by ensuring the right to
   A. access services in French in retail outlets
   B. receive public funds for French education when there are enough students
   C. receive public funds for cultural events that promote the Francophone culture
   D. be hired for a job in an Anglophone setting even if the person applying for the job cannot speak English

8. Which of the following rights is also referred to as a responsibility?
   A. The right to vote
   B. The right to a fair trial
   C. The right to move freely within Canada
   D. The right to make a living in any province or territory

9. Which of the following statements about the Youth Criminal Justice Act (YCJA) is **false**?
   A. Youths under the age of 14 who have committed serious crimes are prohibited from being given an adult sentence.
   B. Some youths may be ordered to undergo counseling instead of incarceration as punishment for their crime.
   C. Young offenders charged under the YCJA will never face a criminal record.
   D. The names of young offenders are not published in the media.

Use the following source to answer the next question.

Examples of Citizen Participation in Canada
I   Voting in an election
II Serving jury duty
III Organizing a demonstration
IV Running for public office

10. Which of the given examples of participation is a responsibility required by law in Canada?
    A. I
    B. II
    C. III
    D. IV

11. Which of the following documents guarantees the collective rights of all Aboriginals in Canada?
    A. Canadian Constitution
    B. Numbered treaties
    C. Bill of Rights
    D. Indian Act

12. The term "status Indian" refers to people in which of the following groups?
    A. First Nations people registered under the Indian Act
    B. Métis people living on Métis settlements
    C. Inuit people living on reserves
    D. All Aboriginal people

13. Which of the following statements regarding immigrant rights in Canada and the Canadian Charter of Rights and Freedoms is **true**?
    A. Only immigrants seeking refugee status are protected by the charter.
    B. There is a separate section of the charter related to the rights of immigrants in Canada.
    C. The rights listed in the charter apply to immigrants as soon as they are on Canadian soil.
    D. Immigrants to Canada are protected by the charter only after they have become citizens.

14. The Canadian government attempts to ensure that each federal constituency
    A. represents a specific ethnic group
    B. includes territory from two or more provinces
    C. contains approximately the same number of voters
    D. groups together citizens with similar political beliefs

15. A group of people who campaign to influence the voting of legislators is called a
    A. lobby
    B. caucus
    C. political party
    D. royal commission

16. Which of the following statements about Canada's federal government reflects an opinion rather than a fact?

    A. The Supreme Court has the power to rule that federal laws are unconstitutional.

    B. Opposition parties should not criticize the decisions and policies of the government.

    C. Members of Parliament are elected in constituencies of roughly equal population.

    D. Cabinet ministers are responsible for government departments.

17. To a supporter of free speech, the danger of having one or two large companies controlling all the major Canadian newspapers is that

    A. news reports may be written with a bias favouring the political views of the owners

    B. the number of subscribers will drop, which will reduce the profits for corporate shareholders

    C. the public will become more aware of the various important issues facing policymakers

    D. information in the newspapers may have to be screened for approval by government censors

18. When it was established, the **primary** role of the Senate was to

    A. provide a second opinion to the House of Commons and help to ensure government decisions were in the best interest of Canadians

    B. veto any decisions made by the government that the Senate believed to be contradictory to the Constitution of Canada

    C. provide royal assent to any bills that have passed through Parliament and are about to become law

    D. decide who has broken the law and what the punishment for the crime should be

19. What is one role of the media during an election?

    A. Instruct citizens about who is the best choice to vote for

    B. Provide information about the platforms of candidates and where to vote

    C. Promote the ideas of candidates who are supportive of democratic ideals

    D. Dissuade citizens from voting for candidates who do not believe in traditional values

20. The responsibility for deciding whether laws and legislation in Canada are constitutional falls to which branch of the government?

    A. Legislative

    B. Provincial

    C. Judicial

    D. Federal

21. Which of the following rights is correctly paired with a corresponding section of Canada's Charter of Rights and Freedoms?

	Right	**Section**
A.	Right to a fair trial	Legal rights
B.	Right to vote in elections	Equality rights
C.	Right to gather together peacefully	Mobility rights
D.	Right to leave Canada	Democratic rights

22. Which three groups have their collective rights guaranteed in Canada?

   A. Immigrants, anglophones, francophones

   B. Francophones, anglophones, aboriginals

   C. Francophones, immigrants, aboriginals

   D. Aboriginals, immigrants, Anglophones

23. Which of the following statements about language rights in Canada is **false**?

   A. All citizens have the right to access federal government services in either French or English.

   B. All citizens have the right to have their children educated in their first language—French, English, or any other.

   C. Within the legal system, all people have the right to an interpreter in the language of their choice if they are unable to understand the proceedings.

   D. When warranted by sufficient number, all citizens have the right to public funds for education in the linguistic minority (either French or English) of a province.

24. Which of the following rights and freedoms from the Charter of Rights and Freedoms does **not** apply to people living in Canada who are not citizens?

   A. Freedom of assembly

   B. The right to enter, remain in, or leave Canada

   C. If convicted of an offense, the right to an expedient trial

   D. The right to be secure from unreasonable search and seizure

25. Which of the following provinces **most strongly** believes that language is of particular importance in immigrant approval?

   A. Alberta

   B. Ontario

   C. Quebec

   D. New Brunswick

26. During which of the following situations would Canada **most likely** increase the number of immigrants it accepts?

   A. Canada is involved in war

   B. Canada's economy is in a boom

   C. Canada's economy is in recession

   D. Canada is facing a natural disaster

ANSWERS AND SOLUTIONS—UNIT TEST

1. C	6. A	11. A	16. B	21. A	26. B
2. A	7. B	12. A	17. A	22. B	
3. A	8. A	13. C	18. A	23. B	
4. A	9. C	14. C	19. B	24. B	
5. D	10. B	15. A	20. C	25. C	

1.   C

The prime minister and his cabinet ministers decide and control which bills will be introduced into Parliament. They generally allow only government bills (which have been designed and approved by members of the cabinet) to be presented to the House. It is usually a cabinet minister who introduces new bills in the House of Commons. Even private members' bills must have cabinet approval before they can be introduced by a member of Parliament.

Bills are rarely, if ever, introduced by a whip or the Speaker in the House of Commons. The Governor General cannot introduce a bill in Parliament.

2.   A

Seventy-five per cent of eligible voters (more than 13.5 million people) regularly cast ballots in election campaigns.

Far fewer Canadians join political parties, run as candidates in elections, or assist candidates with political campaigns.

3.   A

A Canadian senator does not represent a constituency—he or she represents an entire province. Thus, senators are chosen to represent regions. Because each senator from Ontario represents more than 12 million Ontarians, whereas a senator from Prince Edward Island represents only 136 000 islanders, representation by population is obviously not a principle upon which the Canadian Senate is founded. If this principle was at work in the Senate, all senators would represent the same number of Canadian citizens.

Members of Quebec's national assembly, members of Parliament in Canada's House of Commons, and members of legislative assembly in Alberta's legislature all represent a constituency—not a region per se. Moreover, they are elected according to the principle of "one person, one vote" (the principle of representation by population). In other words, each member of national assembly, member of Parliament, or member of legislative assembly represents roughly the same number of constituents as other members of national assembly, members of Parliament, or members of legislative assembly.

4.   A

The right to vote by secret ballot is a political right because it is the way in which citizens choose who represents them in politics.

The right to free speech is a human right, the right to a fair trial is a legal right, and the right to worship as you choose is a cultural right.

5.   D

The legislative branch of the government in Canada consists of the Governor General, the House of Commons, and the Senate. It is the responsibility of these groups to make laws for the country.

The decision about who has broken the law and how criminals will be punished is the responsibility of the judicial branch of the government. Carrying out decisions made by the government is the responsibility of the public service, which is part of the executive branch of government.

6. **A**

    In exchange for the rights provided to citizens, Canadians have certain responsibilities they are asked to perform. In the political process, all eligible Canadians have the responsibility to vote so that the government best represents the desires of society.

    Serving jury duty is considered a legal responsibility. Respecting the rights of others is a moral responsibility, and participating in the community is a social responsibility.

7. **B**

    The charter guarantees that when there are enough students to warrant it, the government must provide funds for French education.

    The charter does not guarantee the right to access services in French in retail outlets, to be guaranteed a job in an Anglophone setting when the person seeking the job cannot speak English, or to receive public funds for cultural events that promote the Francophone culture.

8. **A**

    The right to a fair trial, to move freely within Canada, and to make a living anywhere in Canada are not generally considered to be responsibilities of Canadians.

9. **C**

    Although most youths charged under the YCJA will avoid a criminal record, each case is considered individually. If a youth over the age of 14 has been given an adult sentence, he or she may face a criminal record for life.

    Each of the other three statements about the YCJA are true.

10. **B**

    Citizens are obligated by law to fulfill jury duty if they are called to do so. A citizen can request to be relieved of jury duty but cannot make the decision not to serve themselves.

    Although voting is considered a responsibility, it is not required by Canadian law. Neither organizing a demonstration nor running for office is considered a responsibility of Canadians and is not required by law.

11. **A**

    Under section 35 of the Canadian Constitution, the collective rights of Aboriginal peoples in Canada (including First Nations, Métis, and Inuit) are established.

    The numbered treaties apply only to First Nations peoples. Neither the Bill of Rights nor the Indian Act guarantees the rights of all Aboriginals.

12. **A**

    The term "status Indian" refers to a First Nations person who qualifies to be registered by the federal government.
    There are several qualifications a person must meet in order to be registered and therefore granted the title of "status Indian."

    Neither the Métis nor the Inuit are able to receive this title.

13. **C**

    A ruling by the Supreme Court dictates that the rights listed in the charter are applicable to anyone on Canadian soil, so any immigrant to Canada is protected by the charter as soon as they arrive in the country.

    Immigrants do not have to become citizens to be protected by the charter, immigrant status does not affect a person's ability to be protected by the charter, and there is not a separate section of the charter related to the rights of immigrants.

14. C

Although perfect equality is impossible to achieve, each constituency in Canada contains about the same number of voters. Because of problems with size and some historical distortions, certain constituencies have much smaller numbers of voters than the average.

In Canada, the complex ethnic mix in most communities would make representing a specific ethnic group almost impossible. In order to make representation more meaningful to the voters, constituencies never overlap provincial or territorial boundaries. As a result of the huge variety of opinions, beliefs, and values in Canada, grouping voters on the basis of political beliefs would be impossible.

15. A

A lobby is a group of people who conduct a campaign to influence the voting of legislators.

The term *caucus* refers to a group of elected representatives from the same political party. A political party is a group of people who compete in an election campaign in the attempt to become legislators. A royal commission is an official government inquiry into an area of serious public concern.

16. B

This statement claims that opposition parties "should not" criticize the decisions and policies of the government. This is an opinion. It is the role of opposition parties to watch what the government does and to criticize when necessary. Whether or not they should do so is a matter of opinion.

The other statements are all facts about different branches of the Canadian government.

17. A

A supporter of free speech may be concerned if only one or two large companies controlled all the major Canadian newspapers because this may lead to news reports being written with a bias favouring the political views of the owner. In such a system, the public would have no other alternative sources of news to read in order to obtain a wider perspective on such issues.

Free speech supporters do not suggest that the monopolization of the Canadian newspaper industry will lead to a drop in subscribers, government censorship or a greater awareness of important issues.

18. A

The Senate was formed as a "sober second thought" for the House of Commons. In other words, it was formed as a body that could evaluate decisions made by the government and provide feedback on these decisions.

The Senate has never had veto power over decisions made by the government. The duty of giving royal assent falls to the Governor General (or lieutenant-governor at the provincial level), who is the Queen's representative in Canada. Deciding who has broken the law and handing out appropriate punishments is the responsibility of the Canadian court system.

19. B

The role of the media during an election is to be an impartial source of information for citizens about the beliefs and platforms of candidates. The media also provides election information, such as voting stations and times.

The media should neither instruct nor dissuade citizens to vote a certain way. Although the media sometimes promotes particular ideas through the way these ideas are presented, this is not considered to be an appropriate role of the media during an election.

20. C

The judicial branch of government in Canada is composed of the Supreme Court and its judges. It is their responsibility to decide if legislation is constitutional or not; that is, does it follow the laws of the country and protect the rights of citizens.

Federal and provincial are levels of government, not branches of government. The legislative branch has the responsibility of making and passing law but does not rule on its constitutionality.

21. A

The right to a fair trial is a legal right.

The right to vote in elections is a democratic right (not an equality right). The right to gather together peacefully is a fundamental freedom (not a mobility right). The right to leave Canada is a mobility right (not a democratic right).

22. B

Under the Charter of Rights and Freedoms and Section 35 of the Canadian Constitution, the collective rights of francophones, anglophones, and aboriginals are guaranteed in Canada.

The collective rights of immigrants are not guaranteed in Canada.

23. B

In Canada, all citizens have the right to have their children educated in their first language if it is French or English. The right is not extended to other languages.

Each of the other statements about language rights in Canada is true.

24. B

People who are not citizens of Canada are not granted the right to enter, remain in, or leave Canada, and the government may choose to prevent someone from coming to Canada or force someone to leave Canada.

Each of the other three rights and freedoms are granted to all people in Canada, regardless of citizenship status.

25. C

Because Quebec is concerned about the protection and promotion of the French culture, the province feels it is very important that immigrants are able to speak French and are willing to have their children educated in French.

Although language is a factor for the other three provinces listed, language does not define the culture of those provinces as it does in Quebec.

26. B

Generally, the number of immigrants Canada accepts during an economic boom increases, as there is a greater demand for labour and often not enough people to do the work currently available.

During a recession, immigration tends to slow, as the government does not want to admit people to the country who may not be able to find jobs and may require financial assistance. Both wars and natural disasters tend to slow immigrant acceptance, as the government must deal with the people currently living in the country.

Economic Systems in Canada and the United States

ECONOMIC SYSTEMS IN CANADA AND THE UNITED STATES

Table of Correlations					
Specific Expectation	**Practice Questions**	**Unit Test**	**Practice Test 1**	**Practice Test 2**
Students will:				
Demonstrate an understanding and appreciation of how economic decision making in Canada and the United States impacts quality of life, citizenship and identity				
9.2.4 *compare and contrast the principles and practices of market and mixed economies by exploring and reflecting upon the following questions and issues:* • *What are the principles of a market economy?* • *Why do governments intervene in a market economy?* • *Why is Canada viewed as having a mixed economy?* • *What is the role of the consumer in market and mixed economies?* • *To what extent do consumer actions reflect individual and collective identity?* • *How has the emergence of labour unions impacted market and mixed economies?* • *What are some similarities and differences in the way governments in Canada and the United States intervene in the market economies?* • *How do the economic systems of Canada and the United States differ in answering the basic economic questions of scarcity?*	1, 2, 3, 4, 5, 6	1, 2, 3, 6, 7, 8, 9, 10	18, 23	22, 23, 24, 25, 35, 36
9.2.5 *assess, critically, the relationship between consumerism and quality of life in Canada and the United States by exploring and reflecting upon the following questions and issues:* • *What are the indicators of quality of life?* • *How does individual consumer behaviour impact quality of life?* • *How does marketing impact consumerism?* • *How does consumerism provide opportunities for and limitations on impacting quality of life?* • *How is consumerism used as a power of collective?* • *To what extent do perspectives regarding consumerism, economic growth and quality of life differ regionally in North America?* • *What societal values underlie social programs in Canada and the United States?*	9	5, 14	24, 25, 26, 27, 28, 35, 36, 37	29, 30, 31, 32, 37, 38, 41, 42, 43, 44, 45

| 9.2.6 | assess, critically, the interrelationship between political decisions and economic systems by exploring and reflecting upon the following questions and issues:

• How do the economic platforms of political parties differ from one another?
• How is a political party's philosophy reflected in its platform?
• How does the underground economy impact the federal and provincial tax base and social programs?
• How do government decisions on environmental issues impact quality of life? | 7, 8 | 3, 4, 11, 12, 13 | 19, 20, 21, 22, 38, 39, 40 | 26, 27, 28, 39, 40, 46, 47, 48, 49 |

ECONOMIC SYSTEMS IN CANADA AND THE UNITED STATES

9.2.4 *compare and contrast the principles and practices of market and mixed economies by exploring and reflecting upon the following questions and issues*

THE PRINCIPLES AND PRACTICES OF MARKET AND MIXED ECONOMIES

WHAT ARE THE PRINCIPLES OF A MARKET ECONOMY?

A market economy is one in which decisions about production and prices are based on supply and demand with very little or no government intervention. The belief in the importance of competition, private ownership, efficiency, consumer sovereignty, and the pursuit of self-interest as an incentive for hard work are some of the major principles of a market economy. In this type of economy, people are responsible for their own economic and social well-being and cannot depend on the government to provide services or economic support. Consumers drive the production and prices of goods by the choices they make when spending their money.

FOR WHAT REASON DO GOVERNMENTS INTERVENE IN A MARKET ECONOMY?

Although government involvement in a market economy is extremely limited, governments sometimes intervene to protect consumers with laws, such as those to ensure competition in the market or to prevent price fixing. Governments may also intervene to ensure businesses adhere to minimum ethical practices, such as labour laws or environmental legislation.

FOR WHAT REASON IS CANADA VIEWED AS HAVING A MIXED ECONOMY?

A mixed economy is one in which private ownership and competition are very important, but the government is more heavily involved in a mixed economy than in a market economy. In Canada, most of the economy is privately owned, but the government does have ownership of some industries deemed to be essential to the country. In addition, the Canadian government has more regulations on businesses than would exist in a market economy. Supply and demand are not the only deciding factors for production and pricing in the Canadian economy. The Canadian government also provides services such as welfare and old age pension (among others), which either do not exist or are very limited in a market economy.

WHAT IS THE ROLE OF THE CONSUMER IN MARKET AND MIXED ECONOMIES?

In both market and mixed economies, consumers are the largest driving force for the production of goods. Because most aspects of the markets are privately owned, companies only want to produce what they know they can sell. Consumers drive production by choosing what they will or will not spend their money on, which is known as consumer sovereignty. Consumers can affect the quality and price of products by refusing to purchase something they feel is of low quality or is too expensive. This helps drive competition, as companies try to find the balance between making the highest possible profit from a product but also making sure it is the type and quality of product in demand. Consumers can also influence business practices by refusing to support a company known to abuse labourers or not adhere to environmental standards.

To What Extent Do Consumer Actions Reflect Individual And Collective Identity?

An individual's identity can be reflected through the types of products he or she chooses to buy. For example, different name brands reflect different styles and the stereotypes associated with those styles. As well, a consumer's choice of purchases can reflect his or her values. For example, a consumer who only buys products from fair trade companies is openly expressing that she or he feels fair treatment and payment of labourers is extremely important. A collective identity can be reflected in the same way if a group of people make specific choices about what to purchase.

How Has the Emergence of Labour Unions Impacted Market and Mixed Economies?

A labour union is a group, usually made up of people in a similar industry, that operates to protect and promote the rights of its workers. Labour unions first started to appear in Canada in the late 1800s as a response to difficult working conditions, long hours, and poor pay. The emergence of unions has had a big impact in both market and mixed economies, as industries in which unions exist must make sure that decisions about working conditions and pay coincide with the expectations of the unions. In a mixed economy like Canada, unions have led to changes in government legislation. This legislation protects workers who try to demand change and makes sure people cannot be fired simply for attempting or succeeding to form a union. Supporters of market economies often feel that unions can have a negative effect on the economy, as they demand higher pay for their workers—some people believe that in today's global economy, those jobs can be done more cheaply by workers in foreign countries. In addition, when unions exercise their right to strike, the economy is disrupted, and in some cases, essential services are put on hold.

What are Some Similarities and Differences in the Way Governments in Canada and the United States Intervene in Market Economies?

In both Canada and the United States, the majority of the economy is privately owned and operated. Both governments pass laws to protect the consumer as well as competition in the market. Both set some standards for labour and environmental protection, and both governments provide some form of social services.

Most of the differences between the two governments come from the extent of government involvement in the economy. For example, in Canada, social services are considerably more comprehensive and a broader range of the population can access these services. In the United States, there are fewer social programs and a smaller percentage of the population qualifies for them. In addition, in Canada, certain services deemed essential to the population, such as health care, are regulated and controlled by the federal and provincial governments. Every Canadian citizen can access the health-care system without paying up front. In the United States, citizens pay for their health services either out of pocket or through insurance companies.

Canada has more publicly owned companies (called Crown corporations) than in the United States, although Canada has fewer of these companies now than in the past. These companies are owned by the government to both protect and promote Canada's economy, sovereignty, and cultural identity. Examples of current Crown corporations include the Canadian Broadcasting Corporation (CBC), the Bank of Canada, the Royal Canadian Mint, and Via Rail.

How do the Economic Systems of Canada and the United States Differ in Answering the Basic Economic Question of Scarcity?

Scarcity is an economic condition in which people and society have unlimited wants and needs, but there are limited resources (land, labour, and capital). All types of governments must deal with scarcity, and the way in which they choose to answer the three basic questions involving scarcity dictates the type of economy (market, mixed, or planned) that exists in the country. The three questions are as follows:

- What should be produced?
- How should it be produced?
- Who should have access to the products?

Generally, in the United States and Canada, the questions associated with scarcity are answered through supply and demand. Products or services in demand will be provided through the most efficient means necessary by private enterprise, and those who can afford to pay for them will have access. However, in Canada, more allowance is given to services or products deemed essential. The Canadian government may regulate or outright control the production and distribution of products and services deemed essential to ensure that all people have access, whether or not they can afford to pay.

9.2.5   assess, critically, the relationship between consumerism and quality of life in Canada and the United States by exploring and reflecting upon the following questions and issues

The Relationship Between Consumerism and Quality of Life

What are the Indicators of Quality of Life?

Quality of life is the extent to which a person or group of people is able to achieve well-being. Indicators of quality of life do not only include the extent to which basic needs (such as food, clothing, and shelter) are being met, but other factors as well. Some of these other factors include social or spiritual well-being, such as the ability to speak your own language or practice your chosen religion. In addition, the degree to which a person can access services such as health care, education, and even green spaces can be indicators of quality of life. Political and economic situations, such as the ability to vote or the state of the economy, can also be indicators of quality of life.

How Does Individual Consumer Behaviour Impact Quality of Life?

Consumer behaviour can impact quality of life through the choices consumers make. For example, environmental issues have become much more important in recent decades. Consumers have started demanding that products be more eco-friendly, such as products using less plastic or products being made from materials that can be recycled. Such demands have improved quality of life, as more companies are working to reduce their environmental impact by taking such steps as lowering emissions from their factories, which helps to improve air quality. Consumers are becoming more aware of the impact of waste as landfills fill up and more garbage is found in bodies of water. Often this waste is a result of consumers buying products that are not needed or disposable. Consumers are starting to demand that producers work to reduce waste.

How Does Marketing Impact Consumerism?

Marketing is the way in which companies convey knowledge of their product to the masses and try to influence consumers to buy it. Consumers are bombarded with advertising on billboards, in print, on television and radio, and even on their favourite web page. Marketing can have an immense impact on consumerism as companies try to appeal to consumers in various ways and convince consumers that they should have or use a specific product. Advertising might appeal to a person's ethical values, emotions, or fears, suggest that a product will improve a person's quality of life, or suggest that in order to be accepted in today's society, a person must purchase a specific product. Marketing is a very effective tool for manipulating the behaviour of consumers.

How Does Consumerism Provide Opportunities For and Limitations on Impacting Quality of Life?

Because consumerism is the belief that decisions about production are central to consumer behaviour, consumers have a major impact on their own quality of life through the decisions they make about what or what not to buy. Consumers can provide opportunities for the improvement of quality of life by demanding products that are good for themselves and society. For example, in recent years there has been a push by consumers demanding that food producers reduce or eliminate trans fats from their products. Conversely, consumers can have an adverse effect on their quality of life by buying products even when those products are known to be bad for themselves, society, or the environment.

How is Consumerism Used as a Power of a Collective?

Collective consumerism can be a very effective way for consumers to influence the production, sale, or distribution of a product. Sometimes, groups of people will use boycotts, which encourage the public not to buy certain products in order draw attention to the issue about which they are concerned. For example, the organization PETA (People for the Ethical Treatment of Animals) encourages people not to eat at a certain fast food restaurant because of the way the chickens it uses in its meals are slaughtered.
Other groups concerned with human rights or the environment encourage people not to buy products from companies that have factories set up in countries where the human rights of workers are being abused or the production of products is causing damage to the environment. Through these boycotts, people hope to put enough economic pressure on companies to change their practices.

To What Extent Do Perspectives Regarding Consumerism, Economic Growth, and Quality of Life Differ Regionally in North America?

North America is composed of Canada, the United States, and Mexico. The economies of all three countries vary greatly, yet they are connected through trade agreements and the movement of goods across their borders. Although poverty exists in each of the countries, most citizens in Canada and the United States are generally wealthier than the average citizen in Mexico. As a result, perspectives on consumerism, economic growth, and quality of life are very different in each country. The ability to purchase products that people both need and want effects their belief about the benefits of economic growth as well as quality of life.

What Societal Values Underlie Social Programs in Canada and the United States?

Values demonstrate what a person or society believes to be important. Because of the different economic structures in Canada and the United States, different values are apparent through the ways in which social programs are provided in each country. Both Canada and the United States have systems of social services, but the extent and accessibility of the programs vary greatly between the countries.

In Canada, there is a belief that all people should have equal access to some services deemed essential to the population (such as health care) and that the government has some responsibility to provide for certain groups who may not be able to provide for themselves. As a result, Canada has a universal health-care system supported by both the federal and provincial governments. Under this system, all citizens in Canada can access specific areas of health care without paying out of pocket. In addition, low-income Canadians can apply for further coverage on services that are not publicly funded. Canada also has a pension program for all senior citizens (who have lived in Canada for at least 10 years) as well as programs to support those with physical and mental disabilities.

In the United States, only very low-income earners qualify for publicly funded health care. All other citizens are required to pay for their own health needs or purchase insurance to help with these costs. There is no automatic pension program for senior citizens, and programs for those with disabilities are much more limited than in Canada.

Although this is just an example of some social programs in Canada and the United States, it shows that there is more of a value placed on collectivism (the belief that providing for society as a whole is important) in Canada and on individualism (the belief that people should provide for themselves) in the United States.

9.2.6   assess, critically, the interrelationship between political decisions and economic systems by exploring and reflecting upon the following questions and issues

THE INTERRELATIONSHIP BETWEEN POLITICAL DECISIONS AND ECONOMIC SYSTEMS

HOW DO THE ECONOMIC PLATFORMS OF POLITICAL PARTIES DIFFER FROM ONE ANOTHER?

An economic platform is a description of what policies a political party believes are appropriate to maintain and stimulate the country's economy. It includes policies about taxation, spending, and international economic affairs. Terms often used to summarize a party's platform include right wing, left wing, and centre, which refer to a party's position on the economic spectrum.

Left wing	Centre	Right wing
More government involvement and ownership in the economy, government spending on comprehensive social programs, higher taxes to pay for such services, support for planned economy.	Primarily private ownership with some government intervention and ownership of key industries, medium taxation rates to pay for social services, support for mixed economy.	Less government involvement and ownership in the economy, less spending money on social programs, lower taxes, incentives for big business, support for market economy.

Two of the major political parties in Canada are the Liberal and Conservative parties. On the economic spectrum, the Liberal party is at the centre, and the Conservative party is to the right of centre. As Canada has a mixed economy, parties generally are not considered to be fully left- or right-wing. Generally, some differences between the economic platforms of the Liberal and Conservative parties include the extent to which the government spends money on social programs, rates of taxation, and beliefs about the private versus the public sectors. Generally, the Liberal party supports more spending on social programs than the Conservative party. As an example in regards to taxation, the Conservative party supports more corporate tax cuts than the Liberal party. In addition, the Liberal party is less supportive of private enterprise in areas such as health care than the Conservative party. The Liberal party would likely be more supportive of government spending and regulation to address current issues, such as pollution and other environmental concerns.

It is important to note that Canada has three other parties that are considered mainstream: the New Democratic Party, the Green Party and the Bloc Québécois. The New Democratic Party and the Green Party both support policies considered to be left of centre. The Bloc Québécois exists only in Quebec, but it has an impact on Canadian politics. The Bloc generally supports policies considered left of centre.

In the United States, the two main parties are the Republican and Democratic parties. Although both parties are considered to be right of centre, the Republican party is further right on the spectrum than the Democratic party. Generally, the Democratic party favours more government spending on social programs and would be less likely to cut taxes than the Republican party, which believes more strongly in private enterprise in most areas of the economy. In regards to spending related to global issues, the Democratic party would be more likely to support government regulation and spending to address environmental issues than the Republican party.

How is A Political Party's Philosophy Reflected in its Platform?

The philosophy of a political party can be reflected in its platforms through the policies it makes and the way the party believes government funds should be collected and spent. Policies regarding social programs can reflect whether a political party believes citizens should be able to rely on the government for certain services or if citizens should be responsible for their own well-being. For example, beliefs about welfare spending and eligibility vary between Canada's political parties. Parties who are considered to be more right of centre on the political spectrum generally feel citizens should rely less on the government for their personal well-being. These parties would likely support less government funding and more stringent eligibility guidelines than parties who are more central or slightly left of centre.

Policies about taxes can also be reflected in a party's philosophy. Specific taxes are those such as income tax and the GST. Taxation models are ideas about how much to tax citizens, what goods and services to tax, and how to spend the money that comes to the government in the form of taxes. The policies a party makes in regards to these taxes can be indicative of the party's belief about personal responsibility versus the collective good. Higher taxes generally describe a philosophy in which it is believed that all people should contribute to the welfare of the collective group in society. The government collects more money from citizens through taxation, which then allows the government to spend more on programs for citizens. Conversely, when parties advocate lower taxes, this can reveal a philosophy in which it is believed that people can and should take care of themselves, so taxing citizens less will leave them with more money that they can then use to take care of themselves.

Another example is in the way in which the rates of taxes are charged. A flat tax means that everyone pays the same percentage of tax. For example, Alberta's income tax is a flat tax, meaning all citizens who are required to pay tax are charged the same percentage regardless of how much money they make. Parties supporting this form of taxation likely support wealth as a motivation for hard work, as people are not "punished" in the form of higher taxes for making more money. Progressive taxation occurs when people are charged a higher percentage of tax for making more money. Parties supporting this form of taxation likely support the idea of more support for the collective, as they likely believe people who can afford to pay more tax should do so in order to help those who cannot.

How Does the Underground Economy Impact the Federal and Provincial Tax Base and Social Programs?

Because government income is almost completely reliant on taxation, those who illegally refrain from paying taxes can have a negative impact on government spending. Tax evasion is an illegal practice by which someone does not honestly report how much money she or he made to the government in an effort to pay less tax. The black market is when goods and services are sold illegally, which allows people to either acquire goods not allowed in their country or avoid paying taxes on the goods or services they are buying. The tax base in a country is affected by these practices because all the economic activities and taxes associated with them are not revealed to the government. As a result, the government collects less tax than it should. This can impact social programs because the government has less money to spend and therefore may not be able to support social programs or fund them as much as it could if all the taxes the government was entitled to had been collected.

How do Government Decisions on Environmental Issues Impact Quality of Life?

Because the environment is an important issue, the government's decisions about how to deal with environmental issues can have an impact on the quality of life of Canadian citizens. The government makes decisions that can either work toward the preservation of the environment or the exploitation of it. For example, when the government declares an area of land to be protected by law, it is working to preserve the plants and animals unique to that area. As well, by preventing development of the area, the government may be helping to reduce pollution or preventing the destruction of other important environmental aspects, such as freshwater supplies.

Conversely, government decisions can have the opposite effect and can exploit the environment, which can have a negative effect on citizens' qualities of life. By allowing for development such as the oilsands or more deforestation, the government is allowing for more pollution and the loss of trees and foliage important for cleaning the air. In addition, demand for resources such as lumber and water can result in damage to the environment and the loss of habitats, not only for plants and animals, but also for humans who live in the areas being exploited—this results in serious repercussions for the quality of life of those people.

The trade of natural resources can affect quality of life as well. Because Canada is rich with many natural resources in high demand (e.g., oil, lumber, fresh water), the Canadian government has the potential to make substantial gains through the trade of these resources. Some people believe this improves quality of life, as the government becomes wealthier and is able to spend more on the needs of citizens. Others believe that because of the environmental impact associated with acquiring and converting these resources into marketable products, quality of life is diminished.

PRACTICE QUESTIONS—ECONOMIC SYSTEMS IN CANADA AND THE UNITED STATES

1. In a market economy, the main duty of the government is to

   A. provide services for the poor

   B. prevent the creation of monopolies

   C. establish appropriate environmental standards

   D. allow the economy to operate with a minimum of regulation

2. The role of the consumer in a private enterprise economy is to

   A. provide the demand for products in order to stimulate the economy

   B. make sure that levels of competition are maintained

   C. ensure that consumer goods are of good quality

   D. regulate levels of production

3. The government of a mixed economy would most likely respond to increasing levels of unemployment by

   A. attempting to balance the budget by cutting back government spending

   B. increasing spending on social programs and public works

   C. increasing taxes and raising interest rates

   D. reducing taxes on foreign goods

4. The main purpose of the government in a model free market economy is to

   A. pass laws to protect private property

   B. place tariffs on inexpensive foreign goods

   C. use the taxation system to create income equality

   D. offer financial support to unemployed and low-income citizens

5. In the Canadian mixed economy, there is a significant level of government ownership of

   A. retail stores

   B. alcohol production

   C. health-care facilities

   D. manufacturing production

6. Each of the following economic actions are taken by both the United States and Canadian governments **except**

   A. the provision of social services

   B. the encouragement of competition in the market

   C. the promotion of private ownership in most sectors

   D. the provision of publicly owned and universal health care

7. A political party that favours universal health care, publicly funded daycare, and raising corporate taxes would also likely favour which of the following actions?

   A. Progressive taxation

   B. Private health clinics

   C. Limiting access to social services

   D. Cutting services during tough economic times

8. An example of tax evasion is when someone

   A. accidentally pays more than they owe in taxes

   B. accidentally misses the deadline for submitting a tax return

   C. intentionally pays more tax than required on each paycheque

   D. intentionally misrepresents their income when submitting a tax return

9. Which of the following characteristics is generally not considered to be an indicator of quality of life?

   A. Access to health facilities

   B. Financial well-being

   C. Religious freedom

   D. Political ideology

ANSWERS AND SOLUTIONS—PRACTICE QUESTIONS

1. D	3. B	5. C	7. A	9. D
2. A	4. A	6. D	8. D	

1. **D**

   A pure market system is supposed to operate without government involvement.

   Establishment of environmental standards would be considered by many to be interference in the market system. Unfortunately, in an unregulated market economy, monopolies tend to develop. In a pure market system, the poor are expected to fend for themselves.

2. **A**

   Without the consumer to create demand in a market economy, there would be little or no economic activity.

   Competition between producers is more important than the choices made by consumers in determining the quality of goods. Consumers can help maintain levels of competition in a market economy, but government legislation regulating or outlawing monopolies may be just as important in maintaining levels of competition between businesses. In a market economy, levels of production are determined by the demand for a product.

3. **B**

   Increasing spending on social programs and public works would stimulate the economy and create more jobs.

   Increasing taxes and raising interest rates would create more unemployment by slowing down the economy even more. Reducing government spending would reduce the rate of economic growth and make unemployment worse. Reducing taxes on foreign goods would increase foreign competition and result in more job losses.

4. **A**

   The sanctity of private property and freedom of contract (the right to conclude binding agreements) is essential to the function of a free market economy.

   Interference with the free flow of goods would be a violation of the principles of a free market economy. Advocates of a free market economy do not believe in equality of incomes. Supporters of a free market economy do not believe in aiding the unemployed.

5. **C**

   In a mixed economy, there is a certain amount of government ownership. As a result of embracing the concept of universality (allowing all citizens equal access to the service), the government usually supplies health care.

   In a mixed economy, the ownership of retail stores is usually left in the hands of private businesses. Alcohol production may be regulated, but the actual ownership of the production usually remains in private hands. Manufacturing of goods is usually a function of the private sector in a mixed economy.

6. **D**

   Although universal health care exists in Canada, the United States government does not have ownership of the health-care system, and its services are not universal (available to everyone) as they are in Canada.

   Each of the other actions listed are actions taken by both the American and Canadian governments.

7. A

A political party with the platform described in the question is likely left of centre and would likely support progressive taxation, as it calls for wealthier people to pay a higher percentage of tax.

The party described in the question would not likely support the other actions listed.

8. D

Tax evasion is when a person intentionally misrepresents their income on a tax return in order to pay less or no tax.

None of the other definitions correctly describe tax evasion.

9. D

The beliefs a person holds about politics and the way government should be run generally are not considered to be an indicator of quality of life. Although the ability to express those beliefs may be considered an indicator, just the existence of the beliefs themselves is not.

Access to health facilities, financial well-being, and religious freedom are all considered indicators of quality of life.

UNIT TEST—ECONOMIC SYSTEMS IN CANADA AND THE UNITED STATES

1. Which of the following government actions is **most** characteristic of a mixed economy?

   A. The government allows supply and demand to control the price of both labour and goods.

   B. The government establishes a minimum wage but does not regulate the price of goods.

   C. The government regulates both the supply of labour and the wages workers are paid.

   D. The government regulates wages and prices of goods.

Use the following information to answer the next question.

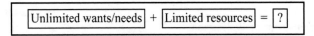

Unlimited wants/needs + Limited resources = ?

2. The question mark in the given equation could **best** be replaced with the term

   A. supply and demand

   B. opportunity cost

   C. consumerism

   D. scarcity

Use the following sources to answer the next two questions.

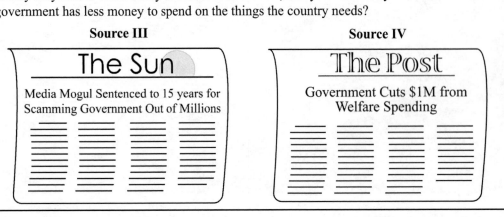

Source I

Brad hid his new DVD under the bed so his parents would not find it. It was pretty cool to have a copy of the latest action flick before it was even released, but he knew his parents would not be happy to hear how he had bought it from some guy at school.

Source II

Matthew watched the news with interest. He could not believe how much money the government believed it was owed by people who did not properly report how much money they made. Didn't they realize that in the end, everyone is hurt by that because the government has less money to spend on the things the country needs?

Source III

The Sun

Media Mogul Sentenced to 15 years for Scamming Government Out of Millions

Source IV

The Post

Government Cuts $1M from Welfare Spending

3. The given source that depicts black market activity is
   A. Source I
   B. Source II
   C. Source III
   D. Source IV

4. The source that depicts a consequence of the other three given sources is
   A. Source I
   B. Source II
   C. Source III
   D. Source IV

5. Which of the following government programs suggests an underlying societal value of individualism?
   A. Progressive taxation
   B. Welfare programs
   C. Public health care
   D. Flat tax rates

6. Which of the following statements is the **most accurate** description of the way the Canadian government deals with goods and services?
   A. The government allows the market to decide what goods and services are provided.
   B. The government and the private sector both provide goods and services.
   C. The government decides what goods and services are provided.
   D. The government provides all goods and services.

7. Which of the following services do the provincial governments of Canada provide to their citizens?
   A. Pharmaceutical supplies
   B. Automobile dealerships
   C. Security guard services
   D. Public schooling

8. If faced with an economic slowdown, which of the following actions would the government of Canada **most likely** take to prevent unemployment?
   A. Reduce government spending
   B. Sell off government-owned businesses
   C. Attempt to stimulate the private sector through tax cuts
   D. Increase the number of government-owned corporations

9. In response to a decline in the value of the Canadian dollar, a government that believes in the values of the market economy would

   A. increase taxes to create a budget surplus

   B. allow the dollar to fall until it stops falling by itself

   C. raise interest rates to encourage foreigners to buy Canadian dollars

   D. lower interest rates to encourage foreigners to sell Canadian dollars

10. In a market economy, low prices, high quality, and innovation are normally a result of

    A. private ownership of land

    B. individual initiative

    C. consumerism

    D. competition

11. Which of the following Canadian political parties would be **most** reluctant to incur a deficit because of increased spending in order to combat a recession?

    A. Liberal party

    B. Conservative party

    C. New Democrat Party

    D. Bloc Québécois Party

12. Which of the following actions would **most likely** have a negative effect on the government's ability to provide social services?

    A. People who underreport their annual income

    B. People who collect support, such as welfare

    C. An increase to the minimum wage

    D. An increase to the income tax rate

13. The purpose of a political party's economic platform is to

    A. inform voters about a party's philosophy surrounding government revenue collection and spending both at home and abroad

    B. inform the public about a party's beliefs about controversial social issues such as the death penalty and abortion laws

    C. instruct voters about where to go to cast their vote on election day and the procedures surrounding voting

    D. provide a forum for discussion about the best way for governments to regulate and monitor the economy

14. Which of the following situations is an example of a boycott?

    A. Hundreds of people signing a letter demanding change to a government policy

    B. Many consumers deciding together not to buy a particular product

    C. People picketing in front of a store to protest its business practices

    D. One country refusing to sell goods to another

ANSWERS AND SOLUTIONS—UNIT TEST

1. B	6. B	11. B
2. D	7. D	12. A
3. A	8. C	13. A
4. D	9. B	14. B
5. D	10. D	

1. B

Minimum wage laws are characteristic of a mixed economy.

Regulation of wages and prices is more characteristic of central planning. Allowing supply and demand to determine wages and prices is characteristic of a market economy. Complete regulation of labour and wages is characteristic of central planning.

2. D

Scarcity is the economic condition that exists when there are limited amounts of land, labour, and capital but unlimited demand for those resources.

Supply and demand is the way the market is regulated when there is little or no government intervention. Opportunity cost is what people sacrifice as a result of scarcity. Consumerism is when consumer behaviour has an impact on economic decision-making.

3. A

Source I describes a young man who bought a pirated DVD, which is part of the black market.

Sources II and III depict tax evasion. Source IV depicts one consequence of tax evasion and the black market—less government income resulting in less government spending.

4. D

Source IV depicts cutbacks in government spending on social programs.

The other three sources depict black market activity and tax evasion, both of which result in less income for the government, which results in less government spending.

5. D

Individualism suggests that people are responsible for themselves and should be rewarded for hard work. A flat tax system means that everyone is taxed at the same rate, as opposed to a progressive tax system, in which people are taxed at a higher rate the more money they make—this is sometimes viewed as a way of punishing those who make more money.

Welfare programs and public health care suggest that the government is taking care of some citizens, which is not a characteristic of individualism.

6. B

In Canada, there is a mixed economy in which the private and public sectors work together to provide goods and services. The private sector is quite large, but the public sector makes sure services deemed essential, such as health and education, are universal.

Although some decisions about goods and services are left to market interplay, the government does make some of those decisions in Canada. The government of Canada does not make all the decisions about goods and services in Canada, nor does it provide all the goods and services.

7. D

Public schools, as the name implies, are considered a government service and are provided by the provincial governments in Canada.

Pharmaceutical supplies are provided to the consumer by private businesses, such as the local drug store. Automobiles are provided to the consumer by privately owned dealerships, such as those that exist in Canada. Security guards are private police forces whose services are contracted out.

8. **C**

Reducing taxes would give the average consumer more spending power, and they would stimulate the private sector, thus creating more jobs.

Privatization of government-owned businesses is not likely to reduce levels of unemployment. This might create a few more jobs if the businesses were run less efficiently, but it is not a good long- or short–term solution. Reducing government spending would increase the level of unemployment.

9. **B**

In a market economy, the government actively controls the money supply. Faced with a falling dollar value, such a government would decrease the money supply to be more in line with demand.

Increasing taxes would likely result in a slowdown in the economy, but would be unlikely to influence the value of the dollar. Raising interest rates would probably increase the value of the dollar, but would interfere in the economy. Lowering interest rates would decrease the value of the dollar even further because of investors selling off the dollar for better investment.

10. **D**

Competition is the overwhelmingly important factor in determining price, quality, and innovation. Without competition, the market economy would not function.

Private ownership of land is an important characteristic of the market economy, but by itself does not affect price, quality, or innovation. Individual initiative is very important in the market economy, but does not necessarily lead to improvements in price and quality or innovation. Consumerism is the desire to acquire goods. It has little or no influence on price, quality, and innovation.

11. **B**

The Conservative party is the most right-wing, mainstream party in Canada, and it would likely rather cut services than increase spending and incur a deficit.

Each of the other three parties would be more likely to incur a deficit through increased spending to combat recession than the Conservative party.

12. **A**

When people underreport the amount of money they made in a year, they likely pay less tax than they should. As taxation is a major source of revenue for the government, that may result in fewer dollars being collected by government and fewer dollars being spent on social services.

An increase to the income tax rate would help the government collect more money and therefore make more money available to be spent on social services. The existence of people who require social services, such as welfare, does not affect the government's ability to provide those services. An increase to the minimum wage would not affect the government's ability to provide social services.

13. **A**

A party's economic platform is an explanation of that party's ideas about how the government should collect and spend money as well as how the country's economy should function in the international community.

None of the other explanations accurately explain the purpose of an economic platform.

14. **B**

A boycott is when many people decide together not to buy a particular product or support a particular company in an effort to convince the company to change its business practices.

Signing a petition and participating in a demonstration are both ways of protesting. When one country refuses to sell goods to another, it is called an embargo.

KEY Strategies for Success on Tests

TEST PREPARATION AND TEST-TAKING SKILLS

THINGS TO CONSIDER WHEN TAKING A TEST

- It is normal to feel anxious before you write a test. You can manage this anxiety by
  - thinking positive thoughts. Imagine yourself doing well on the test.
  - making a conscious effort to relax by taking several slow, deep, controlled breaths. Concentrate on the air going in and out of your body.
- Before you begin the test, ask questions if you are unsure of anything.
- Jot down key words or phrases from any instructions your teacher gives you.
- Look over the entire test to find out the number and kinds of questions on the test.
- Read each question closely and reread if necessary.
- Pay close attention to key vocabulary words. Sometimes these are **bolded** or *italicized*, and they are usually important words in the question.
- If you are putting your answers on an answer sheet, mark your answers carefully. Always print clearly. If you wish to change an answer, erase the mark completely and then ensure your final answer is darker than the one you have erased.
- Use highlighting to note directions, key words, and vocabulary that you find confusing or that are important to answering the question.
- Double-check to make sure you have answered everything before handing in your test.

When taking tests, students often overlook the easy words. Failure to pay close attention to these words can result in an incorrect answer. One way to avoid this is to be aware of these words and to underline, circle, or highlight them while you are taking the test.

Even though some words are easy to understand, they can change the meaning of the entire question, so it is important that you pay attention to them. Here are some examples.

| all | always | most likely | probably | best | not |
| difference | usually | except | most | unlikely | likely |

Example

1. During the race, Susan is **most likely** feeling
   A. sad
   B. weak
   C. scared
   D. determined

HELPFUL STRATEGIES FOR ANSWERING MULTIPLE-CHOICE QUESTIONS

A multiple-choice question gives you some information, and then asks you to select an answer from four choices. Each question has one correct answer. The other answers are distractors, which are incorrect. Below are some strategies to help you when answering multiple-choice questions.

- Quickly skim through the entire test. Find out how many questions there are and plan your time accordingly.

- Read and reread questions carefully. Underline key words and try to think of an answer before looking at the choices.

- If there is a graphic, look at the graphic, read the question, and go back to the graphic. Then, you may want to underline the important information from the question.

- Carefully read the choices. Read the question first and then each answer that goes with it.

- When choosing an answer, try to eliminate those choices that are clearly wrong or do not make sense.

- Some questions may ask you to select the best answer. These questions will always include words like best, most appropriate, or most likely. All of the answers will be correct to some degree, but one of the choices will be better than the others in some way. Carefully read all four choices before choosing the answer you think is the best.

- If you do not know the answer, or if the question does not make sense to you, it is better to guess than to leave it blank.

- Do not spend too much time on any one question. Make a mark (*) beside a difficult question and come back to it later. If you are leaving a question to come back to later, make sure you also leave the space on the answer sheet, if you are using one.

- Remember to go back to the difficult questions at the end of the test; sometimes clues are given throughout the test that will provide you with answers.

- Note any negative words like no or not and be sure your choice fits the question.

- Before changing an answer, be sure you have a very good reason to do so.

- Do not look for patterns on your answer sheet, if you are using one.

HELPFUL STRATEGIES FOR ANSWERING OPEN-RESPONSE QUESTIONS

A written response requires you to respond to a question or directive such as **explain**, **predict**, **list**, **describe**, **show your work**, **solve**, or **calculate.** In preparing for open-response tasks you may wish to:

• Read and reread the question carefully.

• Recognize and pay close attention to directing words such as explain, show your work, and describe.

• Underline key words and phrases that indicate what is required in your answer, such as explain, estimate, answer, calculate, or show your work.

• Write down rough, point-form notes regarding the information you want to include in your answer.

• Think about what you want to say and organize information and ideas in a coherent and concise manner within the time limit you have for the question.

• Be sure to answer every part of the question that is asked.

• Include as much information as you can when you are asked to explain your thinking.

• Include a picture or diagram if it will help to explain your thinking.

• Try to put your final answer to a problem in a complete sentence to be sure it is reasonable.

• Reread your response to ensure you have answered the question.

• Think: does your answer make sense

• Listen: does it sound right?

• Use appropriate subject vocabulary and terms in your response.

TEST PREPARATION COUNTDOWN

If you develop a plan for studying and test preparation, you will perform well on tests.

Here is a general plan to follow seven days before you write a test.

Countdown: 7 Days before the Test

1. Use "Finding Out About the Test" to help you make your own personal test preparation plan.

2. Review the following information:
   - areas to be included on the test
   - types of test items
   - general and specific test tips

3. Start preparing for the test at least 7 days before the test. Develop your test preparation plan and set time aside to prepare and study.

Countdown: 6, 5, 4, 3, 2 Days before the Test

1. Review old homework assignments, quizzes, and tests.

2. Rework problems on quizzes and tests to make sure you still know how to solve them.

3. Correct any errors made on quizzes and tests.

4. Review key concepts, processes, formulas, and vocabulary.

5. Create practice test questions for yourself and then answer them. Work out many sample problems.

Countdown: The Night before the Test

1. The night before the test is for final preparation, which includes reviewing and gathering material needed for the test before going to bed.

2. Most important is getting a good night's rest and knowing you have done everything possible to do well on the test.

Test Day

1. Eat a healthy and nutritious breakfast.

2. Ensure you have all the necessary materials.

3. Think positive thoughts: "I can do this." "I am ready." "I know I can do well."

4. Arrive at your school early so you are not rushing, which can cause you anxiety and stress.

SUMMARY OF HOW TO BE SUCCESSFUL DURING A TEST

You may find some of the following strategies useful for writing a test.

• Take two or three deep breaths to help you relax.

• Read the directions carefully and underline, circle, or highlight any important words.

• Look over the entire test to understand what you will need to do.

• Budget your time.

• Begin with an easy question, or a question you know you can answer correctly, rather than following the numerical question order of the test.

• If you cannot remember how to answer a question, try repeating the deep breathing and physical relaxation activities first. Then, move on to visualization and positive self-talk to get yourself going.

• When answering a question with graphics (pictures, diagrams, tables, or graphs), look at the question carefully.

   – Read the title of the graphic and any key words.

   – Read the test question carefully to figure out what information you need to find in the graphic.

   – Go back to the graphic to find the information you need.

• Write down anything you remember about the subject on the reverse side of your test paper. This activity sometimes helps to remind you that you do know something and you are capable of writing the test.

• Look over your test when you have finished and double-check your answers to be sure you did not forget anything.

PRACTICE TEST 1

Use the following information to answer the next three questions.

Person I

Anna lay awake in her cell, thinking about how glad she was that this was her last night in jail. That stupid mistake a year and a half ago had cost her eight months in this place, and she could not wait to move on. Yes, she had a criminal record, but she was only 23 and ready to change her life for the better. If only she had someone to turn to for some help to get her life back on track.

Person II

Mike hung his head as he listened to the judge give out his sentence. He could not believe his bad luck getting caught stealing those MP3 players. At least the judge was being lenient since Mike had never been caught before and he was only 14—he just had to do a bunch of community service hours.

Person III

John was tired of this life. This is the fourth time in his 35 years of life that he was on his way to jail. He did not know why he kept getting in trouble, but he wanted to make a change. Maybe after he had done his time this time around, he could find a way to get his life going in the right direction.

Person IV

Jill sighed as she watched her latest charge get escorted out of court in handcuffs. As a social worker, she was assigned to accompany lots of young offenders to court if they had no one else to go with them. So many of these kids had such tough lives, it was no wonder they ended up in trouble. At least the justice system seemed to understand that with its legislation that allowed for alternative sentences for kids who just seemed to be on the wrong track.

---

1. Which of the given people would benefit most from contacting the Elizabeth Fry Society?

   A. Person I

   B. Person II

   C. Person III

   D. Person IV

2. The piece of legislation being referred to by Person IV is the
   A. Youth Criminal Justice Act
   B. Criminal Code of Canada
   C. Canadian Constitution
   D. Young Offenders Act

3. Which person in the given source provides the role of advocate within the justice system?
   A. Person I
   B. Person II
   C. Person III
   D. Person IV

Use the following diagram to answer the next question.

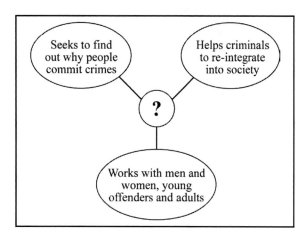

4. The question mark in the given diagram could be replaced with which of the following organizations?
   A. National Parole Board
   B. Elizabeth Fry Society
   C. John Howard Society
   D. Alberta Justice

Use the following information to answer the next two questions.

Speaker I
Canadians can worship at whatever church, synagogue, or temple they choose. They may also choose to be atheists or agnostics and refrain from practicing any religion. In today's world, there are still many countries that persecute people for adhering or not adhering to a particular religion. Canadians are very fortunate that our society and government are tolerant of such a wide variety of religious viewpoints and practices.

Speaker II
Canada rarely, if ever, gets mentioned in the human rights reports of Amnesty International. Why not? Because there are no "prisoners of conscience" in Canada. We do not throw people in jail here because of what they believe, what they say, or who they are. Canadians are worried about many types of crime, but "thought crime" is not one of them. Any Canadian citizen can express his or her ideas in any form he or she wishes—in art, in books, or in a letter to the editor.

Speaker III
One of the greatest things about being a Canadian is that you can complain about the government without fear of arrest, torture, or imprisonment. Imagine having to look over your shoulder before grumbling about Mulroney, Trudeau, or Chrétien. Who would want to live in a country like that?

Speaker IV
In my opinion, freedom of the press is the cornerstone of democracy. In Canada, the media are free to comment and report on any topic they choose. On a daily basis, they criticize the government and pressure it to do better. The media keep our politicians honest.

---

5. All four speakers are referring to
   A. legal rights found in the Charter of Rights and Freedoms
   B. equality rights found in the Charter of Rights and Freedoms
   C. democratic rights found in the Charter of Rights and Freedoms
   D. fundamental freedoms found in the Charter of Rights and Freedoms

6. The speakers neglected to mention that the expression of ideas in Canada is somewhat limited by
   A. pressure groups
   B. slander and libel laws
   C. parliamentary privilege
   D. the unwritten constitution

Use the following information to answer the next question.

> By unspoken agreement, Canadian citizenship carries the ultimate freedom: the freedom to declare that one does not want to be Canadian, to urge that one's region should forthwith cease to be part of Canada, and yet to go on being a Canadian and receiving the appropriate benefits. No Quebec or Alberta separatist, so far as I know, has been denied a federal welfare payment or even a Canada Council grant because of his or her desire to separate.

7. According to the given quotation, the "ultimate freedom" of Canadian citizenship is freedom
   A. to dissent
   B. of speech
   C. of the press
   D. of association

8. Which charter freedom allows Canadian citizens to hold peaceful demonstrations against the government?
   A. Freedom of speech
   B. Freedom of assembly
   C. Freedom of conscience
   D. Freedom of association

Use the following information to answer the next question.

Speaker I
What right does the government have to tell me who I can or cannot get together with in public? Any citizen should have the right to belong to whatever body he or she desires—whether it be a sports team, a quilting circle, or a Neo-Nazi gang.

Speaker II
Any anti-democratic organization should not be tolerated by the federal government. Canada is a democracy. Any group that publicly declares that its objective is to overthrow democracy should be outlawed. Tolerance of such groups disgusts me.

Speaker III
Democracy is about letting people join any political party of their choosing. If we take away this fundamental right, we will be destroying our cherished system of government and the sacred principles upon which it is based. Canada's multiparty system is part of the foundation of its democracy.

Speaker IV
There is a big difference between the YMCA and the KKK. The first is a social organization. The second is a social disease. The last thing we should allow in Canada is the spread of a social disease. It should be a crime to belong to the Ku Klux Klan.

9. Which of the following issues is addressed by all four speakers?

    A. When is it reasonable to limit freedom of assembly for reasons of public security or order?

    B. Are actions taken under the War Measures Act reasonable restrictions on civil liberties?

    C. Should citizens be held responsible for promoting hatred against identifiable groups?

    D. Should limits be placed on freedom of association?

Use the following information to answer the next three questions.

Canadian Legislation Affecting Aboriginals in Canada

Legislation I
Originally passed in 1876, this piece of legislation defines the status of Aboriginals in Canada and dictates the rights and responsibilities associated with that status.

Legislation II
A collection of agreements, these pieces of legislation affect specific groups of First Nations people living in specific areas of the country and defines the rights of the people who are part of those groups.

Legislation III
Existing only in one Canadian province, this grouping of legislations defines eight areas of land over which one Aboriginal group in Canada has certain self-governance rights.

Legislation IV
Affecting all Canadians, this piece of legislation defines the collective rights of Aboriginals in Canada.

---

10. Which of the given pieces of legislation describes the Alberta-Métis Settlements Accord?

    A. Legislation I

    B. Legislation II

    C. Legislation III

    D. Legislation IV

11. The legislation that has resulted in conflicts over rights to land ownership and usage between First Nations and the Canadian government is legislation

    A. Legislation I

    B. Legislation II

    C. Legislation III

    D. Legislation IV

12. Which of the following legislations has been paired correctly with the document to which it refers?

    A. Legislation I—Indian Act

    B. Legislation II—Canadian Constitution

    C. Legislation III—numbered treaties

    D. Legislation IV—Alberta-Métis Settlements Accord

Use the following information to answer the next four questions.

Applicants for Immigration to Canada

David

- Currently resides in Great Britain
- Occupation: computer programmer
- Has no family in Canada
- Once spent time in jail for theft

Chao

- Currently resides in China
- Occupation: investor
- Has family in Vancouver
- Speaks three languages, including English

Falah

- Currently resides in Afghanistan
- Occupation: teacher, but she has been unable to work because she is female
- Frequently faces danger because of war in her country
- Has no family in Canada

Galina

- Currently resides in Ukraine
- Occupation: homemaker
- Has family in Toronto
- Recently diagnosed with HIV

13. Which of the given applicants would **most likely** be considered a security risk to Canada?

   A. David

   B. Chao

   C. Falah

   D. Galina

14. Which of the given applicants would **most likely** have the easiest time being granted approval for immigration?

    A. David

    B. Chao

    C. Falah

    D. Galina

15. Which of the following factors considered by the government when admitting immigrants would **most likely** cause the rejection of Galina?

    A. Economic and political

    B. Health and economic

    C. Political and security

    D. Security and health

16. Which of the given applicants would **most likely** be accepted because of his or her political and humanitarian needs?

    A. David

    B. Chao

    C. Falah

    D. Galina

Use the following source to answer the next question.

Economic Benefits to Canada as a Result of Immigration
I   Larger market
II Larger tax base
III Increased investment
IV Richer cultural diversity

17. Which of the given benefits is incorrectly placed in the list?

    A. I

    B. II

    C. III

    D. IV

Use the following information to answer the next question.

Advantages of the Market Economy

I   A wide variety of goods and services are available.

II There are incentives to use resources efficiently.

III The economy is flexible.

IV Competition results in high quality, low prices, and innovation.

V   Monetary rewards encourage people to work harder and produce more.

18. Which of the following characteristics could be added to the given list?

  A. The economy is subject to the boom and bust cycle.

  B. Consumers can influence the goods and services provided.

  C. The provision of social services ensures equal wealth distribution.

  D. Government regulation ensures good quality products are available.

Use the following information to answer the next two questions.

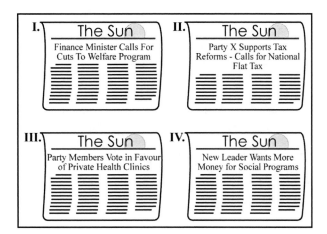

19. The headline that describes an action most likely supported by a left-of-centre party such as the New Democratic Party in Canada is headline

  A. I

  B. II

  C. III

  D. IV

20. The headline that most accurately describes a party whose philosophy includes the belief that the government has a responsibility to support those who cannot provide for themselves is headline

    A. I

    B. II

    C. III

    D. IV

Use the following information to answer the next two questions.

Four Government Actions

I Place a moratorium on fishing for a specific breed of fish

II Approve expansion of an oilsands project

III Assign an area of wilderness as a protected area

IV Increase exports of hard and soft lumber products

---

21. Which of the given actions would be aimed to preserve natural resources?

    A. I and III

    B. I and IV

    C. II and III

    D. II and IV

22. Which of the following statements about the given list of government actions is true?

    A. Each government action works toward the preservation of the environment.

    B. Each government action will increase Canada's gross domestic product.

    C. Each government action is an exploitation of the environment.

    D. Each government action has an impact on the economy.

Use the following cartoon to answer the next question.

"I like robots - they don't join unions, strike or ask for a payrise."

23. What point is being made by the given cartoon?

   A. Robots are more efficient and accurate than people who work on assembly lines.

   B. Unions are important to workers because they provide job security and ensure workers are paid fairly.

   C. From the perspective of an employer, unions cost the company money and are a source of inconvenience.

   D. From the perspective of an employer, unions make it difficult for companies to find workers, so they must develop machines to do the work.

Use the following diagram to answer the next question.

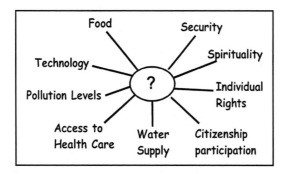

24. The unifying concept in the given diagram is

    A. equity

    B. human rights

    C. quality of life

    D. standard of living

Use the following set of statements to answer the next question.

Statement I
Riches are not from an abundance of worldly goods, but from a contented mind.

Statement II
It is difficult for a man laden with riches to climb the steep path that leads to bliss.

Statement III
A man's life does not consist of the abundance of his possessions.

Statement IV
Excess and deficiency are equally at fault.

---

25. All four of the given statements call for

    A. increased consumerism

    B. restraint in consumption

    C. the eradication of poverty

    D. a greater emphasis on materialism

Use the following cartoon to answer the next question.

"We produce an inferior line of goods, that's why we are looking for a real class marketing person."

26. What statement about marketing is the cartoonist trying to make?

    A. It is difficult to find employees who are skilled in the marketing field.

    B. Employers want to make sure that their marketing employees are quality people with good work ethics.

    C. Marketing can result in consumers being led to believe that products are of higher quality than they actually are.

    D. Marketing is the best way to make sure consumers know that specific lines of products are of especially high quality.

Use the following information to answer the next two questions.

Four Societal Values
I   The importance of the collective
II   The supremacy of the individual
III The value of working hard to support yourself
IV The belief in the importance of helping those in need

27. The two values that contribute to the existence of social programs are

    A. I and II

    B. I and IV

    C. II and III

    D. III and IV

28. The two values that would be considered important in a market economy, such as the one in the United States, are

    A. I and II

    B. I and IV

    C. II and III

    D. III and IV

Use the following statement to answer the next question.

One guiding principle that should be adopted for the protection of human rights is that the state (or collectivity) has its rights delegated to it by the individual. The collectivity is not the bearer of rights; it receives the rights it exercises from the citizens. Citizens should be first of all "equal among themselves." Their rights should take priority over those of the state.

29. The "guiding principle" proposed by the given speaker provides the basis for

A. Aboriginal rights protection

B. the protection of consumers' rights

C. the work of provincial ombudsmen

D. Canada's Charter of Rights and Freedoms

Use the following source to answer the next question.

Two Examples of Human Rights Abuse Complaints

Example I

Sally worked for a large oil company in Fort McMurray. Although she was sometimes intimidated by the fact that she was the only woman on her crew, she knew she did a good job and had never been reprimanded by her boss, although she often felt resented by him. When the job she was doing was suddenly "no longer pertinent" and she was fired, she felt wronged. Later she heard that her position had been "reinstated" and a man had been hired for it. She has launched a human rights complaint saying she was fired because of her gender.

Example II

Aaron is a Jewish man who works in a small grocery store. He asked his boss if he could have a day off to attend Yom Kippur services at his synagogue. Although his boss refused, Aaron did not come into work that day because he wanted to attend services, and he was fired the next time he arrived at work for a shift. He has launched a human rights complaint saying he was fired because of his religion.

---

30. The rights of the people in each of the given scenarios would be protected by which of the following sections of the Charter of Rights and Freedoms?

A. Democratic rights

B. Mobility rights

C. Equality rights

D. Legal rights

Use the following information to answer the next question.

"English and French are the official languages of Canada and have equality of status and equal rights and privileges as to their use in all institutions of the Parliament and government of Canada."

---

31. The given quote was taken from which of the following Canadian documents?

A. The Bill of Rights

B. The Multiculturalism Act

C. The Canadian Constitution

D. The Charter of Rights and Freedoms

Use the following source to answer the next three questions.

Five Views on Canada's Immigration Policies

Speaker I
Immigration is vital not only to the economic health of our country but to one of our fundamental identities—multiculturalism. We Canadians pride ourselves on the fact that people of all races, creeds, and colours can live harmoniously in the same country. Limiting immigration limits our ability to be the best country we can be.

Speaker II
I believe Canada is right to provide safe haven to people from around the world who face persecution. The protection of human rights is very important. However, I believe there are Canadians who, if given the opportunity, could ease the labour shortage and provide the skills and expertise the government seems to think need to come from abroad. Let's make sure Canadians reach their potential first.

Speaker III
Getting into Canada is too easy! I've heard on the news that Canada is known as a safe haven for terrorists because it is so easy to come here, and no one monitors all the foreigners once they are here. We have enough people living here, and the last thing we need is more criminals or people who are plotting against the very thing that makes us who we are—a democracy.

Speaker IV
The reality is my province does not have enough people to fill all the vacant jobs. Drive down any main drag in Edmonton or Calgary and you will count dozens of "help wanted" signs. Obviously, we need more people in our country, or at least this province. Let's open the doors and keep our economy moving!

Speaker V
Sure, multiculturalism is important to Canada, but what about the French culture? Francophones are part of the fabric that built this country, so we need to make sure we protect the language and culture. We need to seek out people who speak French and ensure that they will continue to do so once they arrive. The government must work with Quebecers to make sure this happens.

---

32. The speakers who would support the idea of slowing immigration to Canada are

    A. Speakers I and II

    B. Speakers I and V

    C. Speakers II and III

    D. Speakers III and IV

33. With which of the following factors influencing immigration in Canada is Speaker III **most** concerned?

    A. Economic

    B. Political

    C. Security

    D. Health

34. The speakers who would support allowances for provincial governments to participate in the immigration process are

   A. Speakers I and II

   B. Speakers I and III

   C. Speakers III and IV

   D. Speakers IV and V

Use the following sources to answer the next three questions.

Source I

As a consumer, the choices I make when I buy something have an effect on more than just what I own and how much money I have left. Lately, it has occurred to me that my spending can affect my own well-being by demanding that companies take responsibility for things like pollution, waste, and sustainability. After all, none of us will do well if the air we breathe is killing us. Who knew I had so much power just by going to the mall?

Source II

"New! The Fat Buster Bar! Stop spending Friday night in front of the TV and feel better about yourself when you lose 10 pounds in 6 weeks with the Fat Buster Bar. It's clinically proven to help you lose weight when you use it as a regular meal replacement. Available at most food stores."

"We should try this.
We'll look great by New Year's"

Source III

"Stop the abuse of animals in the name of beauty! Blush Beauty products are tested on animals, causing intense pain in the name of product testing. Make this company change their ways and show your support for these animals by refusing to buy beauty products made by Blush Beauty!"

Source IV

I'm tired of all these companies telling me that I won't have any friends if I don't wear a certain pair of jeans or drink a certain type of pop. As I get older, I am starting to resent a lot of advertising techniques. Companies that just tell me about their product rather than tell me how inadequate I am are the ones whose products I am going to buy!

35. Each of the given sources deals with which of the following issues?

   A. The way in which advertising can affect the spending habits of consumers

   B. The impact advertising has on the self-esteem of young people

   C. The ability of consumers to drive the production of goods

   D. The power consumers have when they band together

36. The source that **best** shows how consumer behaviour can impact quality of life is

    A. Source I

    B. Source II

    C. Source III

    D. Source IV

37. The source that depicts consumers working together as a collective to influence business practices is

    A. Source I

    B. Source II

    C. Source III

    D. Source IV

Use the following source to answer the next three questions.

Four Political Platforms

Platform I
Our party believes that no one should have to pay for services related to their well-being, including health and dental care, or activities and services that benefit all of society, such as post-secondary education. It is the government's responsibility to ensure the economic well-being of its citizens.

Platform II
We believe that as much as possible, people need to be responsible for their own economic well-being. Government handouts and funding for post-secondary education simply cost too much, and the government cannot afford to look after every citizen in this manner. Besides, people are more motivated to work hard when they know no one is going to bail them out.

Platform III
Finding a balance between the government taking care of all aspects of people's lives and leaving it up to citizens to pay for everything they need themselves is what our party is all about. We know there are some things no one should do without, and the government has a responsibility to provide them. However, we also believe citizens must take some responsibility for themselves.

Platform IV
Besides the fact that there are some things in life, such as health care, that should not be restricted based on wealth, the reality is some people cannot look after themselves or provide the necessities of life for themselves. The government cannot turn its back on these people. In addition, sometimes even people who are self-sufficient need a hand, and the government should be able and willing to provide this assistance. Our party believes firmly in this philosophy.

---

38. Which of the given platforms would **most closely** line up with the ideology of the Republican Party in the United States?

    A. Platform I

    B. Platform II

    C. Platform III

    D. Platform IV

39. The two economic platforms that would **most likely** be supported by the Liberal party in Canada are

   A. Platform I and II

   B. Platform I and IV

   C. Platform II and III

   D. Platform III and IV

40. A flat tax for citizens and tax breaks for corporations would **most likely** be supported by a party who also supports the ideas in which of the given platforms?

   A. Platform I

   B. Platform II

   C. Platform III

   D. Platform IV

Use the following quotation to answer the next question.

The theory of collective rights is a dangerous one. For example, if we allow the collective rights of Québécois to dominate, that means Québécois can pretty much ignore the Aboriginal peoples, who say that if Quebec separated, they would not necessarily, join Quebec. The emphasis on collective rights means that large and small collectivities will confront each other in the heart of one and the same country—a situation that can eventually lead to civil wars. That is what collective rights are all about—they enable the collective rights of the majority to abolish the collective rights of the minority. To prevent this from happening, we must always favour another category of rights over collective rights.

41. The speaker of the given quotation would **most strongly** oppose the

   A. protection of fundamental freedoms

   B. principle of legal equality between citizens

   C. recognition of Quebec as a distinct society in the Constitution

   D. protection of the minority rights of Aboriginal peoples in Quebec

Use the following quotation to answer the next question.

Today, a Canadian citizenship certificate is a coveted prize among people born in countries where civil rights are limited or non-existent. It formally guarantees freedom of religion, expression, and lawful assembly and freedom from discrimination on the basis of gender, ethnic origin, or disability. This certificate and the phrase "citizen of Canada" both excite admiration and envy throughout the world.

42. The given quotation suggests that foreigners view Canadian citizenship as desirable **mainly** because of

   A. cultural reasons

   B. political reasons

   C. personal reasons

   D. economic reasons

Use the following sources to answer the next three questions.

Source I

Canada—Permanent Immigrants by Category—1983-2007 (Select Years)

Category	1983	1993	2003	2007
Family Class	48 942	112 667	65 112	66 230
Economic Immigrants	24 187	105 662	121 045	131 248
Refugees	13 969	30 623	25 984	27 956
Other Immigrants	2 094	7 751	9 207	11 323

Source II

Immigrants to Canada tend to have a high level of education. 38% of male workers with a post-graduate degree are immigrants to the country. 49% of doctorate holders and 40% of those with a master's degree were born outside Canada. All of this is due to the fact that the Canadian system puts great emphasis on finding skilled immigrants.

43. The immigration trends in Source I show

   A. Family Class immigrant numbers have risen then fallen while Economic Immigrant numbers have risen.

   B. Family Class Immigrants have risen while Economic Immigrant numbers have fallen.

   C. Refugee numbers have risen then fallen while Family Class Immigrants have fallen.

   D. Refugee numbers have fallen while Other Immigrant numbers have risen.

44. According to the information in Source II which type of immigrant is the Canadian government looking for?

   A. physically fit

   B. family focused

   C. highly educated

   D. financially secure

45. The two sources support the view that the Canadian Government is seeking which category of immigrant?

    A. Family Class Immigrants

    B. Economic Immigrants

    C. Refugee Immigrants

    D. Other Immigrants

Use the following source to answer the next three questions.

Views on the Senate

Speaker 1
The Canadian Senate is important because the senators make sure all the regions of Canada have an equal voice.

Speaker 2
The Canadian Senate has no use. It is a place for retired politicians who slow down the work of the duly elected Members of Parliament.

Speaker 3
Senators provide a chamber of sober second thought for bills from the House of Commons. They make sure that laws are made to benefit everyone.

Speaker 4
Senators are not representative of the people because they are appointed and not elected. This is not fair.

---

46. The ideas presented by Speakers 2 and 4 highlight the

    A. role of political parties in Canada

    B. importance of the head of state of Canada

    C. division of power in Canada's government

    D. need to reform a branch of Canada's government

47. Which two speakers believe that the Canadian Senate is a valuable part of the Canadian political system?

    A. Speakers 1 and 3

    B Speakers 2 and 4

    C. Speakers 1 and 4

    D. Speakers 2 and 3

48. The main issue of the information in the source is whether or not

    A. divergent views of Canada's Senate exist among citizens

    B. similar views of Canada's Senate are held by all citizens

    C. the senate should be changed

    D. the senate should be elected

Use the following source to answer the next question.

Title _____
• Hired by a group of influential MPs and government officials
• Must register with a special commissioner so everyone in Canada knows who they are and who they represent
• Must document which MPs and government officials they meet with

49. The **best** title of the list above is

    A. Citizen's Use of Lobbyists

    B. How are Lobbyists Administered by Government

    C. What are the Roles and Responsibilities of Lobbyists

    D. The Ways Lobbyists make Governments Respond to Citizens

Use the following diagram to answer the next question.

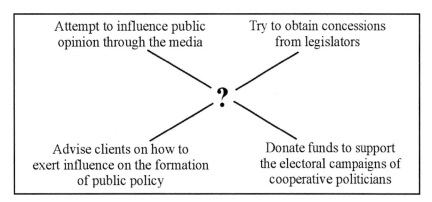

50. Which of the following terms belongs at the centre of the given diagram?

    A. Petitioners

    B. Lobby groups

    C. Demonstrators

    D. Political parties

ANSWERS AND SOLUTIONS—PRACTICE TEST 1

1. A	11. B	21. A	31. D	41. C
2. A	12. A	22. D	32. C	42. B
3. D	13. A	23. C	33. C	43. A
4. C	14. B	24. C	34. D	44. C
5. D	15. B	25. B	35. C	45. B
6. B	16. C	26. C	36. A	46. D
7. A	17. D	27. B	37. C	47. A
8. B	18. B	28. C	38. B	48. A
9. D	19. D	29. D	39. D	49. C
10. C	20. D	30. C	40. B	50. B

1. A

Person I is a woman who is about to be released from prison. The Elizabeth Fry Society helps women and girls who have been convicted of crimes get help and re-integrate into society.

As people II and III are male, they would not be helped by the Elizabeth Fry Society. Person IV has not committed a crime and therefore does not require the Elizabeth Fry Society.

2. A

The Youth Criminal Justice Act is the piece of legislation that deals with young offenders in Canada. A major goal of the act is to rehabilitate young offenders and find alternative punishments to incarceration for certain crimes.

The Young Offenders Act was replaced by the Youth Criminal Justice Act. The Criminal Code of Canada applies to crimes committed by adults. The Canadian Constitution does not deal with laws surrounding criminal acts.

3. D

Person IV is a social worker who works on behalf of and advocates for young offenders.

The other three people in the given source are people who would benefit from someone advocating on their behalf.

4. C

The John Howard Society is an organization that is separate from the government that works to find out why youths and adults commit crimes. The society helps to rehabilitate those who are re-integrating into society.

The Elizabeth Fry Society is a similar organization, but it works only with women and girls convicted of crimes. The National Parole Board decides if criminals will be allowed parole or not and does not help criminals re-integrate into society. Alberta Justice is part of the provincial government, and although it may direct people to organizations like the John Howard Society, it does not do the work the society does.

5. D

All four speakers are referring to fundamental freedoms identified in Canada's Charter of Rights and Freedoms. Speaker I refers to freedom of religion. Speakers II and III mention freedoms of thought, belief, opinion, and expression. Speaker IV mentions freedom of the press.

None of the four speakers mention legal, equality, or democratic rights.

6. B

Slander (making false and damaging oral statements about someone) and libel (presenting false and damaging ideas about someone in written words, printed words, or pictures) are illegal actions in Canada. Slander and libel laws are meant to protect a person from having his or her good reputation injured by false and malicious accusations. Freedom of expression does not give a citizen the right to violate the rights of others by defaming them.

Pressure groups (interest groups) are important vehicles of free expression; they do not serve to restrict free speech. Parliamentary privilege is a special right enjoyed by members of Parliament in the House of Commons. This privilege gives members of Parliament immunity from libel and slander charges for whatever they say within the House of Commons chamber. This allows members of Parliament greater freedom of expression than ordinary citizens and is meant to allow for the freer debate and discussion of public issues in the legislative assembly. This privilege certainly does not serve to limit free expression. The unwritten constitution (the traditional rules for running the country) does not serve to limit the free expression of ideas. Furthermore, slander and libel laws are statute laws, not constitutional laws.

7. A

The given quotation suggests that the freedom to dissent (the freedom to disagree with the government and to criticize it) is the ultimate democratic freedom.

The quotation does not deal as directly with the other freedoms (the freedoms of speech, the press, and association) as it does with the freedom to dissent. Dissent implies disagreement with and rejection of the established system of government.

8. B

Freedom of assembly allows people to gather together in groups for non-violent and non-criminal purposes. This freedom makes it possible for people to hold public demonstrations against the government.

Free speech, freedom of conscience, and freedom of association (the freedom to form political parties and other organizations) are not as essential as the freedom of assembly for the staging of a demonstration against the government.

9. D

All four speakers are responding to the question "Should limits be placed on the freedom of association?" Freedom of association refers to the freedom of citizens to organize themselves into a group for a joint purpose.

All the speakers do not address the three other questions. For instance, they do not specifically discuss the freedom of assembly (the right of people to gather together in a group for a public meeting, demonstration, rally, etc.).

10. C

The Alberta-Métis Settlements Accord is a collection of legislation aimed to provide autonomy and economic self-sufficiency for the Métis. There are no other agreements like it in Canada.

Legislation I is describing the Indian Act. Legislation II is describing the numbered treaties. Legislation IV is describing the Canadian Constitution.

11. B

Legislation II is describing the numbered treaties, under which the right to land ownership and usage for First Nations people is listed. However, in recent decades there have been conflicts between First Nations and the Canadian government (with whom the treaties are signed) as to the modern-day application of these rights.

Legislation I is describing the Indian Act. Legislation III is describing the Alberta-Métis Settlements Accord. Legislation IV is describing the Canadian Constitution.

12. A

Legislation I is describing characteristics of the Indian Act.

Legislation II is describing the numbered treaties. Legislation III is describing the Alberta-Métis Settlements Accord. Legislation IV is describing the Canadian Constitution.

13. A

David has a criminal record, and therefore may be considered a risk to Canada. Generally, the government does not approve immigration of convicted criminals.

None of the other applicants have characteristics that would be cause for them to be considered a security risk.

14. B

Chao would be able to contribute to the Canadian economy, as he has money for investments, he is able to speak one of the official languages in Canada, and he has family already in Canada who would likely be able to help him settle.

David's criminal record would make it difficult for him to immigrate. Although Falah is well-trained, her lack of family to help her transition to Canada may make it more difficult for her to immigrate. Galina's illness may make it more difficult for her to immigrate, as the Canadian government does not want to admit people who may put a strain on the health-care system.

15. B

Immigrant applicants with very serious illnesses requiring intensive treatments and drug therapies are sometimes rejected, as they would put an unreasonable strain on Canada's health-care system. Economics may also impact her application, as she is currently not working outside the home in her own country. In addition, her ability to work in Canada may be inhibited by her health issues.

Galina's application suggests she is neither a political refugee nor a potential security risk to Canada

16. C

Falah lives in a country where there is currently a war being fought, and she has been discriminated against because of her gender. The Canadian government would likely approve her application as a refugee based on political factors.

None of the other applicants face similar political situations in their home countries.

17. D

Although richer cultural diversity is considered to be an advantage to Canada as a result of immigration, it is not an economic benefit— rather, it is a social one.

Each of the other three benefits listed are economic benefits for Canada.

18. B

The influence of consumers in a market economy is considered an advantage because producers are accountable to the consumer and must make products of sufficient quality, which are desired by consumers, or their business will not survive. Therefore, the consumer is able to access good quality goods that they want to buy.

In a market economy, there are neither government regulations nor the provision of social services. The boom and bust cycle of the market economy is generally not considered to be an advantage but rather a disadvantage, as it results in instability in the market.

19. D

The New Democratic Party in Canada believes that the government has a responsibility to provide for citizens who have difficulty providing for themselves and would therefore likely support an increase in funding for social programs.

None of the other actions described in the headlines would likely be supported by the New Democratic Party.

20. D

Headline IV suggests that the government should spend more money on social programs, which are ways the government helps to support citizens who need help for various reasons. These programs include welfare, employment insurance, and old age pensions, among others.

Headline I is the opposite of Headline IV, as it is suggesting the government reduce its spending on social programs, thereby limiting its responsibility to support citizens.

Headline II suggests that all people should pay the same rate of tax, regardless of how much money they make. This is likely an action not supported by a party that believes in government support of citizens, as that party would likely support progressive taxation in which the wealthy pay a higher rate of tax. Headline III suggests that the government relinquish some of its control of the health-care system by allowing private clinics. This would likely not be supported by a party such as the one in the question, as this provision would result in people with more money being able to pay for potentially better health services and receive care faster than those with less money.

21. A

Placing a moratorium on fishing would prevent people from fishing for a particular species and allow it to increase it numbers. Assigning an area of wilderness as a protected area ensures that no development or exploitation will take place there, preserving the natural habitat that exists in that area.

Government actions II and IV would reduce or deplete natural resources rather then preserve them.

22. D

Each of the actions listed in the source will have an impact on the economy because each action will either increase the profit made from resources (actions II and IV) or limit the growth of profit from resources (actions I and III).

Actions II and IV do not work to preserve the environment, but rather to exploit it. Actions I and III do not exploit the environment, but rather preserve it. Actions I and III will likely not increase Canada's gross domestic product.

23. C

The caption of the cartoon is being spoken from the perspective of a business owner who is saying that unions cost the company money through pay raises for employees as well losing money through strikes. Both pay raises and strikes cost the company money and are a big inconvenience for the company.

The cartoon does not comment on the ability of robots versus people to do work. The cartoon does not discuss the importance of unions to workers. The cartoon does not suggest that unions are the source of labour shortages.

24. C

All of the factors listed affect quality of life (the general level of happiness of a society).

The concepts of equity (justice or fairness), human rights, and standard of living (the material wealth of a society) do not provide a unifying link for the diagram.

25. B

All four of the given statements are highly critical of consumerism; all of them call for restraint in consumption (limiting the amount of goods and services that people consume).

The given statements call for decreased—not increased—consumerism and materialism. Only Statement IV calls for the eradication of poverty.

26. C

The cartoonist is suggesting that if marketing is done well, consumers will think a product is of higher quality than it really is because they will believe the advertising.

The cartoon does not discuss the difficulties of hiring marketing employees. The cartoon suggests that companies are not concerned with the work ethics of their employees. The cartoon does not discuss the ability of marketing to make sure consumers are aware of the quality of a specific line of products.

27. B

Social programs are based on the idea that some people need help to provide for themselves and both government and society have a responsibility to provide for those people. Placing value in the collective and helping those in need are two values rooted in the provision of social programs.

Values II and III place more importance on individuals being responsible for themselves, which is not the basis of the provision of social programs.

28. C

In a market economy, such as that in the United States, individualism and hard work are core values. In such an economy, people are responsible for themselves and are expected to provide for themselves through hard work.

Values I and IV suggest a mixed economy, in which there is less emphasis on the individual and more on the collective.

29. D

The guiding principle mentioned in the given quotation—the idea that "the state has its rights delegated to it by the individual"—is the basis for Canada's Charter of Rights and Freedoms. The charter is founded upon the idea that the protection of individual rights must take precedence over the protection of collective (group) rights and the rights of the state (government).

It is clear that the given quotation is referring to a category of human rights that is broader than Aboriginal collective rights, consumer rights, or the right to fair treatment by the provincial government.

30. C

Under section 15 (equality rights) of the charter, citizens are protected from discrimination based on both religion and gender. Both cases would be protected by this section.

Human rights claims based on discrimination would not be protected by the democratic rights, mobility rights, or legal rights sections of the charter.

31. D

The quote is taken from section 16 (1) of the Charter of Rights and Freedoms, which guarantees equality between Canada's official languages—French and English.

Although the charter is entrenched in the Constitution, this quote was taken from the charter itself. Neither the Bill of Rights nor the Multiculturalism Act includes this quote.

32. C

Speaker II suggests that immigration is limiting the potential of Canadian workers, and Speaker III suggests that immigration is dangerous for Canadian security. Both speakers feel the government should limit immigration.

Speaker I suggests that immigration is important to Canada's identity, and Speaker IV suggests immigration is important to Canada's economy. Speaker V suggests immigration is important to preserving the French culture.

33. C

Speaker III is concerned with the security of the nation, as she or he suggests that criminals and terrorists are too easily permitted to immigrate to Canada—this creates a threat to Canadian security.

Speaker III does not address issues surrounding politics, economics, or health.

34. D

Speaker IV suggests that each province may have individual needs for immigration based on the economy in that province. Speaker V suggests that Quebec should be involved to ensure some immigration is geared to protecting the French culture.

Neither speakers I, II, nor III suggests provincial involvement in the immigration process is important.

35. C

Each of the given sources depicts a scenario in which consumers demonstrate how they can manipulate the production of a product—either through buying it or refusing to buy it.

The self-esteem of young people, the collective action of consumers, and the effect of advertising on spending habits are not depicted in the given sources.

36. A

Source I shows how by deciding to buy or not to buy products based on their environmental records can improve quality of life by reducing pollution and improving the environment.

Sources II and IV describe how advertising can influence consumer choice. Source III shows how consumers working as a collective can influence the business practices of companies.

37. C

Source III depicts an organization concerned with animal rights calling on consumers to boycott (refuse to buy) products from a particular company in order to influence the company to change its product testing procedures.

Neither Source I, Source II, nor Source IV describes consumers working as a collective.

38. B

Platform II describes a right-wing philosophy in which government financial assistance to citizens is limited and citizens are primarily responsible for their own economic well-being. The Republican Party in the United States is a right-wing party and would likely support this platform.

Each of the other platforms describe philosophies that are not closely in line with the philosophy of the Republican Party.

39. D

The Liberal Party of Canada is considered to be in the centre of the economic spectrum and is supportive of Canada's mixed economy. The Liberal party believes in the importance of self-sufficiency but also has policies that allow for government support for social programs for those who are in need and other areas deemed essential for all citizens.

Platform I would be considered too left-wing for the Liberal party, and platform II would be considered too right-wing for the Liberal party

40. B

A flat tax and tax breaks for corporations are often supported by parties with a right-wing philosophy, which is described in platform II.

Likely, parties who support the philosophies of platforms I, III, and IV would not support a flat tax system and tax breaks for corporations.

41. C

The speaker in the given quotation is against the granting of collective rights (special protections for a particular group). He or she would most strongly oppose the recognition of Quebec as a distinct society in the Constitution. The speaker would do so because he or she feels that it would lead to special rights and privileges for Quebecers that would not be enjoyed by other citizens.

The speaker is opposed to protecting the rights of a group. He or she favours a society in which no citizen enjoys a right that is not enjoyed by every other citizen.

42. B

The term *political* describes anything related to the state or its government. The quotation suggests that the Canadian government's recognition of democratic rights and freedoms is what makes Canada an attractive destination for immigrants from other countries.

43. A

The interpretation of the information, analyzing of the information , and sorting of the information demonstrates that the trend of immigrants in Canada is that Family Class immigrant numbers have risen then fallen while Economic Immigrant numbers have risen.

44. C

The information provided in Source II focuses on the concept of education. It speaks to post-graduate degrees and doctorates. It clearly states that the Canadian system places great value in education.

45. B

Both sources point to the value in skilled and educated immigrants and the greatest increase in number of immigrants is shown in Economic Immigrants.

46. D

The focus of the two speakers is the need to reform the Senate, which is a branch of Canada's government.

47. A

Speakers 1 and 3 show common characteristics within their ideas focusing on the Canadian Senate being a valuable part of the Canadian Political System.

48. A

The information in the source clearly demonstrates that very different views of the value of the Canadian Senate exist among citizens in Canada.

49. C

The list provided describes who and what lobbyists and lobby groups are therefore the best title is "What are the Roles and Responsibilities of Lobbyists?".

50. B

All four descriptions can only describe lobbyists (people who conduct a campaign to influence the voting of legislators).

Petitioners, demonstrators, and political parties do not advise clients about how to influence the formation of public policy. These groups do not have clients (customers or people who use the services of a professional person).

PRACTICE TEST 2

Use the following diagram to answer the next question.

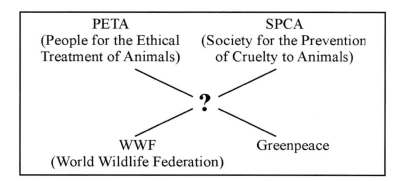

1. Which of the following terms **best** completes the given diagram?

   A. Lobby groups

   B. Extremist groups

   C. Consumer groups

   D. Environmental groups

Use the following information to answer the next question.

Governments in Canada increasingly make use of mass media to promote their plans and new policies. Unfortunately, when they do this, they simply employ the run-of-the-mill techniques of commercial advertising. Their announcements do not seek to inform or educate the public. Rather than providing sufficient information or a balanced view of an issue, they merely use simple repetitive messages, feel-good slogans, and slick images to influence and manipulate. Using the media in this way is blatantly antidemocratic.

2. The given quotation suggests that government announcements in Canada's mass media are

   A. illegal

   B. informative

   C. propagandistic

   D. unconstitutional

Use the following information to answer the next three questions.

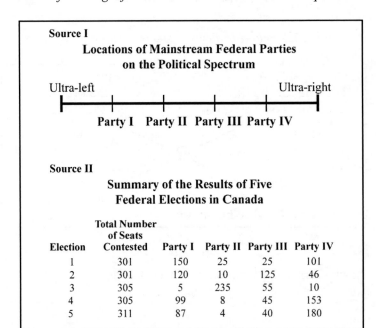

3. During its five-year term of office, which party most likely governed the country **least** effectively?

   A. Party I

   B. Party II

   C. Party III

   D. Party IV

4. If the members of all four political parties are ideologically inflexible, the coalition cabinet formed after Election 1 most likely contained members from parties

   A. I and II

   B. I and III

   C. I and IV

   D. II, III, and IV

5. A minority government resulted from elections

   A. 1 and 2

   B. 1 and 4

   C. 2 and 3

   D. 2 and 4

Use the following information to answer the next two questions.

Legal Responsibilities in Canada
I Knowing the law
II Constructing the law
III Following the law
IV Obeying the law

6. Which of the given responsibilities does not apply to all people in Canada?

   A. Responsibility I

   B. Responsibility II

   C. Responsibility III

   D. Responsibility IV

7. If someone is arrested, claiming ignorance about the law she or he has been accused of breaking is not a defence permitted by Canada's justice system, as it contradicts which of the given responsibilities?

   A. Responsibility I

   B. Responsibility II

   C. Responsibility III

   D. Responsibility IV

Use the following information to answer the next three questions.

8. In the given cartoon, Judicial Man **most likely** represents

    A. the RCMP

    B. the federal cabinet

    C. government lawyers

    D. the Supreme Court of Canada

9. What weapon could Parliament Man or Provincial Man use to effectively stop the most controversial of Judicial Man's lawful actions?

    A. Closure

    B. The War Measures Act

    C. The notwithstanding clause

    D. The Criminal Code of Canada

10. What is the source of Judicial Man's extraordinary new powers?

    A. The BNA Act

    B. The amending formula

    C. The unwritten constitution

    D. The constitutional protection of civil rights

Use the following information to answer the next question.

"Since 1982, the protection of rights in Canada has taken a whole new direction. Entrenched in the constitution, covering a wide scope and used as the benchmark for everything from religious expression to job security, Canada's rights legislation has had a massive impact on our society."

11. The piece of legislation being discussed in the given quote is the Canadian

    A. Constitution

    B. Bill of Rights

    C. Criminal Code

    D. Charter of Rights and Freedoms

Use the following information to answer the next three questions.

Scenario I
A woman discovers that her male co-worker, who has the same job description as she does, receives higher pay than her.

Scenario II
A man is fired from his job after his boss learns that he is 63 years old. The man suspects his age is the reason for his termination.

Scenario III
A recent immigrant arrives at a polling station on election day but is denied a ballot.

Scenario IV
A teenager has her backpack searched by a teacher who suspects she has drugs inside it.

---

12. Which of the given scenarios could not be challenged as a violation of individual rights protected by the Charter of Rights and Freedoms?

    A. Scenario I

    B. Scenario II

    C. Scenario III

    D. Scenario IV

13. Scenarios I and II could both be challenged under which section of the Charter of Rights and Freedoms?

    A. Fundamental freedoms

    B. Democratic rights

    C. Equality rights

    D. Legal rights

14. The scenario that depicts a potential abuse of the rights in the legal rights section of the charter is

    A Scenario I

    B. Scenario II

    C. Scenario III

    D. Scenario IV

Use the following information to answer the next question.

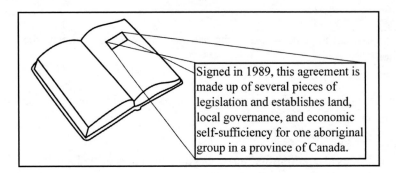

Signed in 1989, this agreement is made up of several pieces of legislation and establishes land, local governance, and economic self-sufficiency for one aboriginal group in a province of Canada.

15. The given passage is referring to which of the following documents?

   A. Indian Act

   B. Numbered treaties

   C. Canadian Constitution

   D. Alberta-Métis Settlements Accord

Use the following information to answer the next question.

A Francophone family living in Alberta is unable to access a Francophone school for their children in their town.

16. The given source depicts a scenario dealing with which of the following rights in the Charter of Rights and Freedoms?

   A. Equality rights

   B. Collective rights

   C. Individual rights

   D. Democratic rights

Use the following information to answer the next question.

Potential Benefits to Canada from Immigration

• Cultural diversity

• Promotion of human rights

• Economic growth

17. Which of the following benefits could be added to the given list?

   A. Domestic security

   B. Lower crime levels

   C. Decreased population growth

   D. Promoting the minority official language

Use the following information to answer the next four questions.

Andy

My grandfather immigrated to Canada from Hungary in 1956 when he was 20 years old. At the time, the Communist government in Hungary was very oppressive and treated dissidents like my grandfather very harshly. He found refuge in Canada and was able to openly express his views about the way the government treated people in his homeland to make the world aware of what was going on there.

Mike

My great-grandfather left his wife and three children at home to come to Canada to help build the railroad. He was assigned to some of the most dangerous work, blasting through the mountains with dynamite. After the railroad was completed, he wanted to bring his family here to live with him. There was so much red tape, and he was forced to pay a head tax for each of them to come for no other reason than their race.

Sam

My parents and I immigrated here in 2003 from Rwanda. No one asked us about our religious views or the colour of our skin. Mostly, the government was concerned that we were healthy and that my parents would be able to get a job fairly easily. It probably helped that my dad is educated as an engineer and we speak French.

Elie

Sometimes I can hardly believe the stories my grandmother tells me about trying to come to Canada during the Second World War. As Jews, they were persecuted in Europe, and her parents wanted to bring them somewhere safe. They got on a boat to come to Canada but were turned away and had to go back because the government did not think the persecution of Jews was a Canadian problem. Luckily, she survived Hitler, although no one else in her family did.

---

18. The speaker who has benefitted the **most** from the changes to the Immigration Act that make Canada's immigration policies more inclusive is

   A. Andy

   B. Mike

   C. Sam

   D. Elie

19. From which country were Mike's ancestors **most likely** trying to immigrate to Canada?

    A. South Africa

    B. Mexico

    C. Britain

    D. China

20. Which of the given speakers describes Canada's attempt to criticize international political policy through immigration?

    A. Andy

    B. Mike

    C. Sam

    D. Elie

21. Taken together, the given speakers demonstrate

    A. the way Canada's immigration policies have evolved to reflect world issues

    B. Canada's past and continued commitment to the promotion of human rights

    C. Canada's reluctance to allow people of varying races to immigrate to Canada

    D. how historically and in the present, Canada has been a safe haven for refugees

Use the following information to answer the next question.

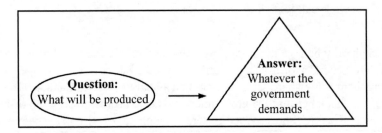

22. The given answer provided is **most closely** followed in a nation with a

    A. mixed economy

    B. market economy

    C. capitalist economy

    D. centrally planned economy

Use the following information to answer the next question.

Beliefs of a Market Economy
I   Consumers should have as wide a range of product choice as possible.
II   Private ownership of the nation's resources is necessary.
III There must be competition between producers in the marketplace.
IV Equal distribution of incomes is essential.

23. The belief that has been incorrectly included in the given list is belief

   A. I

   B. II

   C. III

   D. IV

Use the following information to answer the next two questions.

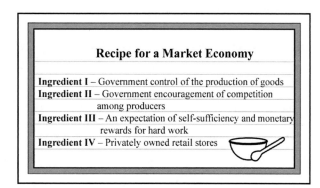

24. Which of the ingredients is **incorrectly** included in the given recipe?

   A. Ingredient I

   B. Ingredient II

   C. Ingredient III

   D. Ingredient IV

25. Which of the following ingredients could be correctly added to the given recipe?

   A. Government ownership of the means of production

   B. Publicly funded post-secondary education

   C. Consumer sovereignty and choice

   D. Belief in collectivism

Use the following information to answer the next question.

> When Federal Fisheries Minister John Crosbie arrives in Newfoundland on Canada Day, he's looking for a joyous Confederation celebration. Instead, he's met by a furious crowd of fishermen, plant workers and their families. They hold brown cardboard placards and taunt him: "Is this the best you can do, buddy?" The group is angry because tomorrow Crosbie will place a moratorium on fishing Atlantic cod, which represents their livelihood. That means no more work for at least 20,000 inshore fishery workers. The industry has supported rural Newfoundlanders for more than 400 years. And the province's infrastructure relies on it—everyone from truck drivers to grocery store owners will be affected.
>
> —*from* cbc.ca

26. The excerpt in the given source is describing
    A. the environmental impact of overfishing in Newfoundland
    B. the historical importance cod fishing has to the culture of Newfoundlanders
    C. the potential impact on quality of life as a result of government decisions about the environment
    D. the successful protest by Newfoundland fishermen at preventing a potentially economically devastating decision by the government

Use the following information to answer the next two questions.

Some Economic Decisions Made by the Government

I Increase spending on pensions for senior citizens

II Sell off previously government-owned corporations

III Reduce regulations in the economy

IV Provide more grants for post-secondary education

27. Which two of the given decisions would be characteristic of the Republican Party in the United States?
    A. Decisions I and II
    B. Decisions I and IV
    C. Decisions II and III
    D. Decisions III and IV

28. Which two of the given decisions would be characteristic of the Democratic Party in the United States?
    A. Decisions I and II
    B. Decisions I and IV
    C. Decisions II and III
    D. Decisions III and IV

Use the following source to answer the next two questions.

> It is time North American consumers clued in to the fact that it is their habits that are the cause of the massive environmental damage being done every day. Our insatiable taste for bottled water, our head-in-the-sand attitude about throwing stuff out, and our belief that we "need" a car the size of a bus is resulting in damage that soon, if we do not do something about it, will be irreversible.

29. The speaker is suggesting that consumer behaviour

    A. is not something that can be changed

    B. has a positive effect on the environment

    C. has a negative effect on the environment

    D. is something that varies between regions in North America

30. When the speaker mentions consumers' beliefs that they "need" a car, he is **most likely** referring to a dependence on which of the following industries?

    A. Manufacturing

    B. Forestry

    C. Retail

    D. Oil

Use the following source to answer the next two questions.

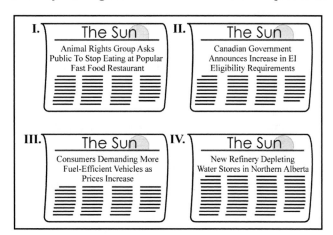

31. The headline that is depicting a boycott is headline

    A. I

    B. II

    C. III

    D. IV

32. Headline II suggests that Canada's social policies

    A. reflect a belief that people are responsible for their own financial well-being

    B. suggest the government is responsible to provide some support to citizens

    C. aim to make people accountable for their own behaviour while at work

    D. are not sufficient for the number of people who require them

Use the following information to answer the next two questions.

Consider the following examples of people who have immigrated to Canada.

Scenario I
A young Japanese woman who has studied computer engineering and has a job with a large Toronto firm.

Scenario II
The wife and three children of a Rwandan man who immigrated three years prior.

Scenario III
A Chinese man who has received death threats for expressing his anti-government political views.

Scenario IV
A wealthy British entrepreneur who has recently expanded his business into Canada.

---

33. Which of the given scenarios is the best example of Canada expressing its views about human rights through immigration?

    A. Scenario I

    B. Scenario II

    C. Scenario III

    D. Scenario IV

34. The two scenarios that describe people who were permitted to immigrate mainly because of their potential to be an economic benefit for Canada are scenarios

    A. I and II

    B. I and IV

    C. II and III

    D. III and IV

Use the following information to answer the next three questions.

Case Study I

Jim Flobber reluctantly closed and locked the door of his small hardware store for the last time. He sighed. He had made a decent living for 15 years, but then that huge chain store had moved in only three blocks away. Folks that used to come to his store drove right by on their way to that gigantic store. There was absolutely no way that his business could survive.

Case Study II

Mrs. Ko and her husband arrived in Canada in 1986. They both acquired jobs as kitchen helpers in a small restaurant. By 1989, they had saved enough money to open a small restaurant of their own. In 1993, they started a janitorial service and expanded their restaurant. By 1998, their two businesses employed 25 people and brought in a clear profit of $200 000 each year. When interviewed by a local newspaper about her amazing success, Mrs. Ko said, "It's not hard to make money in Canada. You just have to work."

Case Study III

Bob Apples noticed that in the last two years, a large number of small landscaping businesses had opened up. Believing he was entering an expanding market, Bob spent his life's savings on a pickup truck and landscaping equipment. The business, however, did not take off as expected. He found that even when he offered discounted rates, there was not much need for his services. The problem was that there were simply too many other people doing the same job.

Case Study IV

"The problem with snow blowers," said Bill Clarke, "is that all they do is blow snow. The rest of the year, they just sit. I have developed a machine that can blow snow in the winter, rototill gardens in the spring, and mow lawns in the summer. My machine costs only 20% more than a single snow blower. So far, I have two big lawnmower firms bidding for the rights to my invention."

Case Study V

Frank Chan counted out the day's receipts. Another pretty good day. He had been quite concerned when that enormous discount store had moved into town two years ago, but he had found a way to compete. The big store could always outdo him for prices, but big stores do not repair their products when they break. He had simply gone into the appliance- and machine-repair business. He had even contacted the manager of the discount store to let him know what he was doing. The discount store sent him a lot of business. It was easier for the big store to let Frank repair its defective merchandise than to set up its own repair shop.

---

35. The principle of a market economy that is illustrated in Case Study I is

    A. competition

    B. individualism

    C. supply and demand

    D. private ownership of the means of production

36. The free market principle of rewarding hard work is most clearly illustrated in

    A. Case Study I

    B. Case Study II

    C. Case Study III

    D. Case Study IV

37. One principle of free enterprise that is illustrated by Case Study II is

    A. public ownership

    B. freedom of choice

    C. supply and demand

    D. individual initiative

Use the following sources to answer the next three questions.

Source I

The weakness of a mixed economy is that it does not leave entrepreneurs the freedom they require to adequately stimulate the economy. Instead, those people engaged in business are frustrated in their efforts by a tangle of government regulations and unnecessary restrictions. As a result, those nations that emphasize free enterprise develop much more rapidly than those that hamper the efforts of the true capitalist.

Source II

The economies of countries that give free rein to capitalists develop more rapidly. There is ample statistical data to support this claim. However, there is a price to be paid for this rapid development and economic freedom. First of all, the lack of regulation in a pure market economy results in serious damage to the environment. In addition, there is a human price to pay as workers are exploited so that a few aggressive individuals can enrich themselves.

Source III

The concept of an unregulated free enterprise system often sounds appealing, as those who favour such a system praise its advantages and point out the tiresome burdens of government regulation. However, in a modern economic system, government regulation is essential if consumers are to be protected against unscrupulous business practices. Imagine a society in which consumers were totally at the mercy of the entrepreneur. How many shoddy and even dangerous products would be passed off onto the unsuspecting buyer?

Source IV

What is required in a modern economy is not an absence of government regulations, but a system in which the business community is free to create new wealth while being controlled by safeguards that protect society in general. Such a society would ensure that consumers and workers are protected from the perils of unregulated capitalism. In addition, the average citizen would share in the wealth created by the entrepreneurial class.

---

38. The issue of concern in all of the given sources is

    A. protecting workers from the hazards of capitalism

    B. the most effective way to stimulate the modern economy

    C. finding an economic system that is the most capable of creating wealth

    D. the extent to which the government should involve itself in the economy

39. The accusation that a mixed economy stifles the efforts of entrepreneurs is made in Source

    A. Source I

    B. Source II

    C. Source III

    D. Source IV

40. The given sources that are supportive of a mixed economy do so on the grounds that a mixed economy

    A. is more effective at generating wealth than a market economy

    B. prevents businessmen from making too much money

    C. eliminates poverty and promotes equality

    D. provides for the protection of the public

Use the following source to answer the next three questions.

Scenario I

Sam and Max stood at the back window of the plastics plant they both worked in. "I can't believe no one complains about that," Max said as he gazed out at the greenish-black goo flowing out of a pipe from the factory into the river.

"People do all the time! I overheard the boss say that our company has been taken to court for all the pollution it causes."

"How come nothing ever changes?" Max asked.

"Well," shrugged Sam, "it's cheaper for them to just pay the government's fine then spend the money to clean up their act."

"Wow." Max said.

"Yup. Well, our lunch break is over—back to the old grind!"

Scenario II

"In other news, tire-producing giant Terrific Tires has drastically changed their production methods, bowing to consumer pressure. Over the past 12 months, the environmental group GreenNOW! has engaged in a public campaign asking people not to buy tires from Terrific Tires because of the high levels of pollution from their Canadian tire factories. Because of this campaign, the company has seen their sales drop over 10%."

Scenario III

Megan was frustrated. It seemed like hardly anyone really cared about how their individual actions had an impact on the environment. She wished people could understand that if everyone made small changes and realized how much power they had just by opening their wallets, they could see huge changes in the way companies did business.

Scenario IV

Sandi could not believe how easy it was for her company to make some changes and decrease their environmental footprint. Installing the equipment did not cost as much as she had thought, and she had saved lots of money by using less energy and water. Not to mention the fact that they would get some good press for the work they had done, which would help sales, and her company would get some much needed tax breaks from the government.

---

41. Which of the given scenarios demonstrates consumerism being used as a collective to exact change in business practices?

   A. Scenario I

   B. Scenario II

   C. Scenario III

   D. Scenario IV

42. Which scenario suggests that the government has not done enough to promote positive environmental business practices?

   A. Scenario I

   B. Scenario II

   C. Scenario III

   D. Scenario IV

43. Each of the given scenarios suggest that consumer behaviour can have an effect on business practices **except**

   A. Scenario I

   B. Scenario II

   C. Scenario III

   D. Scenario IV

Use the following cartoon to answer the next two questions.

"Gentlemen, we have a dilemma. Pollution scientists say it will destroy the ozone - however, Market Research predict it will sell like hot cakes."

44. The "dilemma" being suggested in the given cartoon is if

    A. consumers will buy a product that will be damaging to the environment

    B. the company should advertise that their new product is potentially damaging to the environment

    C. the company should choose profit over environmental protection when deciding what products to sell

    D. consumers will boycott the company for selling products they know to be environmentally dangerous

45. The **main** point being made by the cartoonist is that companies

    A. often have difficulty making decisions about what products will be profitable once they are marketed

    B. are always reluctant to produce products that may be harmful to the environment

    C. can find it difficult to balance environmental responsibility with profit-making

    D. with good environmental practices usually make products that sell very well

Use the following source to answer the next three questions.

Profiles of Canadian Voters

Gary

I believe that Canadians should look out for each other. Governments should spend more money on programs like welfare and look out for our senior citizens. We should use progressive taxation to make sure that those who can afford to pay a little more do and those who need every penny they make can save a bit.

Shannon

Although I think there are some people who need the government's help, most people can and should look after themselves. That being said, I do think the government should spend money on welfare, and some things like health care and education should be universal because it should not be just the rich people who get the good doctors and teachers. I also like the progressive taxation system.

Paul

Government handouts make people lazy. People should have to work for what they get, and if they are successful, they should not be punished by having to pay more tax. Also, running a deficit is simply an irresponsible way to govern—my vote goes to the party that will cut spending and be fiscally responsible.

Lynn

Although I know my opinion is not popular, I still believe strongly that the government really knows what is best for its citizens and should have the most say in the day-to-day workings of the country's economy. Government regulation is the only way to make sure that everyone gets what they need and that the gap between rich and poor is not too great.

---

46. Which Canadian political party would Shannon **most likely** support in an election?

    A. Liberal

    B. Republican

    C. Democratic

    D. Conservative

47. Which two voters would likely support political parties that are on opposite sides of the economic spectrum?

    A. Paul and Lynn

    B. Lynn and Gary

    C. Paul and Shannon

    D. Shannon and Gary

48. Corporate tax breaks and the selling of Crown corporations to private owners would be actions **most likely** supported by which voter?

    A. Gary

    B. Shannon

    C. Paul

    D. Lynn

49. The term that refers to not reporting income to the government to avoid paying the required taxes is called

    A. tax write off

    B. tax evasion

    C. tax bracket

    D. tax return

ANSWERS AND SOLUTIONS—PRACTICE TEST 2

1. A	11. D	21. A	31. A	41. B
2. C	12. C	22. D	32. B	42. A
3. B	13. C	23. D	33. C	43. A
4. A	14. D	24. A	34. B	44. C
5. A	15. D	25. C	35. A	45. C
6. B	16. B	26. C	36. B	46. A
7. A	17. D	27. C	37. D	47. A
8. D	18. C	28. B	38. D	48. C
9. C	19. D	29. C	39. A	49. B
10. D	20. A	30. D	40. D	

1. **A**

   A lobby group (or pressure group) is an organization that tries to pressure the government to adopt its recommendations. PETA, the SPCA, the WWF, and Greenpeace all try to do this.

   Extremist groups are groups that advocate the use of violence or employ violent or criminal methods to achieve their objectives; the SPCA, WWF, and Greenpeace do not use such methods in the pursuit of their goals. Consumer groups are organizations that seek to protect buyers from being cheated by manufacturers, sellers, and distributors. The given groups are not consumer groups. Environmental groups are organizations that attempt to protect nature from being destroyed by human pollution and development. PETA and the SPCA are not environmental groups.

2. **C**

   Propaganda refers to any attempt to influence a person's views through a simple, one-sided, non-rational, and emotional message. The given quotation suggests that the government in Canada regularly uses such messages to influence the citizenry to believe what the government wants them to believe.

   The quotation does not suggest that government announcements are illegal, informative, or unconstitutional.

3. **B**

   Party II lost 227 of its 235 seats after its term of office.

   No other party suffered such strong voter disapproval after its period in power.

4. **A**

   If a party is ideologically inflexible, it means that it will have difficulty working with parties from other parts of the political spectrum. The further away a party is from the ideologically inflexible party on the spectrum, the lesser the chance of the two parties being able to work together. The most likely coalition government would be formed by Party I and Party II, as these two parties are closer on the political spectrum than the other parties that could make up other possible coalition governments.

   Even though parties II, III, and IV could form a coalition government made up of 151 of the 301 members of Parliament, there is little chance that ideologically inflexible Party II could work together with ideologically inflexible Party IV, which is so far away from it on the political spectrum.

5. **A**

A minority government is formed whenever the party that wins the most seats in the House of Commons does not hold a majority of the seats. This happened in both elections 1 and 2, when no party won the minimum number of seats (50% of the seats plus one) required to form a majority government. The minimum requirement would have been 151 of 301 seats.

Elections 3 and 4 resulted in majority governments.

6. **B**

The responsibility of constructing the law falls to Canada's elected officials in the House of Commons and members of the Senate.

Each of the other responsibilities listed applies to all people in Canada.

7. **A**

To claim ignorance is to say that a person does not know the law, which is one of the responsibilities listed. People in Canada may not use ignorance of the law as a defence.

Claiming ignorance is not related to constructing, following, or obeying the law.

8. **D**

Judicial Man most likely represents the highest court in Canada—the Supreme Court. This court has been the main target of Canadian complaints about "judicial activism."

The RCMP, cabinet members, and government lawyers work for the executive branch of government, not the judicial branch.

9. **C**

The notwithstanding clause is the part of Canada's Constitution that allows the federal government and the provincial governments to override the rights guaranteed in Canada's Charter of Rights and Freedoms. This clause could be invoked by a government to thwart court decisions.

Closure is a procedure for prematurely ending the debate of a controversial bill in a federal or provincial legislature. It stifles opposition in the legislature, but it does nothing to curtail the power of the courts. The War Measures Act temporarily suspends the rights of citizens, but it can only be invoked by the prime minister and the federal cabinet—provincial politicians, by themselves, cannot proclaim it. The Criminal Code of Canada is a federal statute that defines which actions are criminal offences in Canada and sets the limits for punishments of convicted criminals. The code could not be used to stop a judge or court that is lawfully exercising its responsibilities.

10. **D**

The Charter of Rights and Freedoms is the section of the Constitution that protects the civil rights of Canadians. The charter is the source of the judiciary's new powers. Since the charter came into effect, judges have sometimes interpreted the charter in ways unforeseen by the legislators who created it. In recent years, the courts have used the charter to strike down several provincial and federal laws that were deemed to violate charter rights and freedoms.

The BNA Act and the unwritten constitution have existed since the time of Confederation (1867) and as such, could not be responsible for the recent ascent of judicial power in Canada's democracy. A new amending formula (procedure for making changes to the Constitution) appeared in Canada's Constitution in 1982, but this formula gave no additional powers to the Canadian courts.

11. **D**

The given quote describes legislation that is entrenched in the Constitution and has been in existence since 1982—this describes the Charter of Rights and Freedoms.

The Bill of Rights was not entrenched in the Constitution, and it was passed in 1960. Although the charter is part of the Constitution, the quote is describing the charter itself. The Criminal Code deals with what is considered a crime in Canada and what the potential punishments are for that crime.

12. C

Because the right to vote is extended only to Canadian citizens, a new immigrant would not be allowed to cast a ballot.

Scenarios I and II could be challenged under the equality rights section of the charter. Scenario IV could be challenged under the legal rights section of the charter.

13. C

Under the equality rights section of the charter, it states that people may not be discriminated against based on age or gender.

Discrimination based on age or gender is not addressed in any other section of the charter.

14. D

Under the legal rights section of the charter, all people are protected against unreasonable search and seizure.

None of the other scenarios depict situations that would be relevant to the legal rights section of the charter.

15. D

The Alberta-Métis Settlements Accord is a land claim agreement that sets out the regulations for the Métis settlements in Alberta. On these settlements, the Métis have local governance, ownership of the land, and economic self-sufficiency. These settlements are the only ones like this in Canada.

The given quote is not describing the Indian Act, the numbered treaties, or the Canadian Constitution.

16. B

Collective rights apply to a group of people, and in Canada, these collective rights are provided to anglophones, francophones, and aboriginals. Because the source depicts the plight of a francophone family, the rights associated with francophones in Canada would apply.

The source is not relevant to individual rights, equality rights, or democratic rights in Canada.

17. D

The Canadian government can use immigration to promote the minority official language (French) in Canada by seeking immigrants who speak the language and want to continue to do so as well as to educate their children in that language. By having more people in the country who speak that language, it helps to promote and preserve it, which is especially important to francophones and the province of Quebec.

Domestic security is not intentionally affected by immigration and is not viewed as a benefit. Immigration increases rather decreases the population. Lower crime levels is not related to immigration.

18. C

Sam describes how his family was able to immigrate to Canada based on qualities such as their economic potential and the fact that they speak French. Race and religion were not factors, which is part of Canada's immigration policy.

Each of the other speakers describes race or religion as a factor in their difficulties immigrating to Canada. Over time, Canada has responded to world issues, such as the promotion of human rights, to make its immigration policies and laws inclusive.

19. D

Many Chinese men came to Canada to do very dangerous work building the CPR. After the railroad was finished, many wanted to bring their families to Canada, but the Canadian government introduced a head tax on Chinese immigrants as a way to discourage Chinese people from immigrating to Canada.

People from Britain, South Africa, and Mexico were not subjected to such treatment.

20. A

Andy describes how his grandfather was able to immigrate to Canada from a Communist country. During the 1950s, there was great tension between Communist and democratic countries, and one way of condemning the actions of Communist countries was for Canada to allow the immigration of people deemed dissidents in those countries.

None of the other speakers describe such scenarios.

21. A

The speakers depict various times in history and Canada's immigration policies at those times. Historically, Canada was more discriminating and less concerned with how immigration policies reflected the values of Canadians. The speakers show how Canada's policies have evolved and changed over time.

Not all the sources demonstrate a reluctance to allow people of varying races into Canada. Elie describes how Canada has not always been a safe haven for refugees. Both Mike and Elie describe how Canada has not always had a commitment to the promotion of human rights.

22. D

A centrally planned economy is almost completely government-controlled.

A mixed economy would answer the question with "Whatever consumers demand and whatever the government chooses to provide as services." A capitalist economy would answer the question with "Whatever consumers demand." A free market economy is the same as a capitalist economy.

23. D

An equal distribution of incomes is a characteristic of a Communist economy, not a capitalist one.

Capitalists believe that the economy thrives by allowing entrepreneurs to make and keep profits.

24. A

In a market economy, the government does not control the production of goods. Production is driven by consumer demand and what will be profitable in the market.

A market economy encourages competition, invites an expectation of self-sufficiency and provides monetary rewards, and allows for privately owned retail stores.

25. C

In a market economy, consumers have control over what they buy. Consumers are provided with choices because various producers exist and provide a variety of products at varying quality and prices.

Each of the other ingredients in the list would not exist in a market economy.

26. C

The excerpt is describing how the government's decision to place a moratorium on cod fishing in Newfoundland has a potentially devastating effect to Newfoundland's economy and therefore to the quality of life for Newfoundlanders.

The excerpt does not discuss the impact of overfishing or the historical importance of cod fishing in Newfoundland. Although the excerpt describes a protest, the excerpt does not suggest that the protesters were successful in reversing the decision about the moratorium.

27. C

Typically, the American Republican party has supported less government intervention in the economy, so selling government-owned businesses and reducing regulations would fit with the party's ideology.

The party would be less likely to increase social spending or provide more funding for post-secondary education, as part of the party's ideology is an expectation that citizens should look after their own economic health.

28. B

Typically, the Democratic party in the United States is more supportive of providing for citizens in need and would likely support increased funding for seniors and post-secondary education.

The party would likely not be supportive of selling government-owned businesses and reducing regulations.

29. C

The speaker suggests that many consumer habits are causing damage to the environment and that these habits need to change or the environmental damage will be permanent.

The speaker does not suggest that consumer behaviour has a positive effect on the environment and suggests that the behaviour can and should change. The speaker does not discuss regional differences in consumer behaviour.

30. D

One of the major issues facing North America in terms of vehicle habits is the huge dependence on the oil industry in order to fuel the millions of vehicles in North America and the fact that the majority of those vehicles are large SUVs or trucks that require a large amount of gasoline.

Although the car industry also includes the manufacturing and retail industries, those are not likely the ones causing the environmental damage described by the speaker. The forestry industry is not related to the damage being done by vehicles.

31. A

A boycott is when people do not buy a product or support a company in an effort to cause financial hardship for that company so that they will change their habits or policies. Headline I is calling for people to stop eating at a particular restaurant, which would be a boycott of that restaurant.

None of the other headlines depict a boycott.

32. B

By increasing the eligibility requirements for the employment insurance program as Headline II suggests, the government is demonstrating its responsibility to provide support to citizens who are in need of financial help, such as those who have been laid off from their jobs and need financial assistance.

Such a policy does not suggest that people are responsible for their own well-being or that people must be accountable for their behaviour at work. The headline does not discuss the sufficiency of Canada's social programs.

33. C

Canada believes strongly in the right to voice dissenting political views. Allowing the man who has been targeted for doing so to immigrate to Canada is a way for Canada to display its belief in human rights.

Both scenarios I and IV are examples of people who will likely bring economic benefit to Canada through their immigration. Scenario II demonstrates Canada's commitment to humanitarianism through reuniting families.

34. B

Both people described in scenarios I and IV will likely be able to contribute to Canada's economic well-being because of their knowledge and wealth.

Although the people described in scenarios II and III may very well contribute to Canada's economy, that was not likely the main reason they were permitted to immigrate.

35. A

Competition is the force in a market economy that creates better products, better prices, and better services. Businesses that cannot compete are driven out of business.

The principle of supply and demand controls the pricing of goods in a market economy. Case Study I is an example of a businessman failing because of superior competition. Individualism is what makes people set up their own businesses in an effort to succeed. Case Study I does not emphasize individualism as much as it emphasizes the factor of competition. Case Study I does illustrate private ownership, but it is not emphasized as the main idea of the study.

36. B

Case Study II most clearly illustrates that hard work can lead to success.

The emphasis in Case Study I is on the effects of competition—it illustrates the problems a small businessman has when facing competition from a larger competitor. The emphasis in Case Study III is also on competition, but this case illustrates the effects of oversupply on a business.
Case Study IV emphasizes innovation.

37. D

Hard work and individual initiative—the willingness to take matters into one's own hands—is illustrated in Case Study II.

Case Study II does not illustrate supply and demand, it illustrates that hard work and determination can lead to success.
Public ownership refers to government-owned businesses. There is no hint of that in Case Study II. Freedom of choice is a phrase that is usually applied to consumers of goods and services rather than to those who supply them.

38. D

The main source of disagreement between the given sources is whether or not the government should involve itself in the regulation of a market economy.

None of the sources are concerned about stimulating the economy. Source I is definitely not concerned about the welfare of workers. None of the sources are in disagreement about the system that best creates wealth.

39. A

Source I accuses the government of frustrating business with "a tangle of government regulations."

The writer of Source II believes that government regulation is necessary to protect the environment and the worker. The writer of Source III believes government regulation is necessary to protect the consumer. The writer of Source IV believes government regulation is necessary to provide adequate safeguards to society.

40. D

Sources II, III, and IV all claim that government regulation will protect the public in some way.

None of the sources are in favour of reducing the levels of profit of the business community.
Only Source IV claims that government regulation will promote equality.

41. B

Scenario II explains how a public boycott of a tire company because of their pollution record caused the company to change their practices in order to stop losing money and bring consumers back.

None of the other scenarios explain the work of a consumer collective.

42. A

Scenario I describes how it is cheaper for a company with a poor environmental record to pay the fines for pollution than to take the needed steps to improve their pollution record.

Scenarios II and III do not deal with government involvement in environment legislation. Scenario IV depicts government tax breaks as an incentive for a company to improve their pollution record.

43. A

Scenario I does not refer to consumerism in any way.

Scenario II depicts the power of a boycott. Scenario III suggests people could demand change through what they choose to buy or not to buy. Scenario IV describes a business owner who hopes consumers will support her company as a result of the efforts she has made to become more environmentally friendly.

44. C

The caption suggests that even though the product is known to be harmful to the environment, the company will likely make money by selling it. The dilemma is whether or not to sell a product that is harmful to the environment, even though it will make money for the company.

The cartoon does not refer to advertising for the product. The cartoon suggests that consumers will buy the product even though it is harmful to the environment, so that is not a dilemma for the businessmen. The cartoon does not suggest a boycott by consumers.

45. C

The cartoonist suggests that the potential for making money can make it difficult for companies to practise environmental responsibility. If they know a product will sell, they may be tempted to put it on the market even if they know it is damaging to the environment.

The cartoonist does not suggest that companies have difficulty making marketing decisions, that they are always reluctant to make products that are damaging to the environment, or that companies with good environmental practices make popular products.

46. A

The Liberal Party of Canada is supportive of some social programs but also believes in individualism. The Liberal party is supportive of universal health care and education and favours progressive taxation.

The Conservative party would likely spend less on social programs than would be supported by Shannon. The Republican and Democratic parties are American political parties.

47. A

Paul supports a party that would not want much government intervention in the economy and would expect people to ensure their own economic well-being. Lynn supports a party that believes in extensive government intervention and ensuring equality among citizens. Paul's party would be considered right wing, while Lynn's party would be considered left wing.

The parties supported by Shannon and Gary would be closer to the centre of the political spectrum than the other two.

48. C

Paul supports right-wing economics and low government involvement in the economy, which are values that underlie actions like corporate tax breaks and privatization.

Gary, Shannon, and Lynn would be less likely to support such actions, as their political beliefs are more central and left wing.

49. B

Tax evasion is when someone does not report part or all of his or her income in an effort to avoid paying the required taxes. The government is not aware of how much money he or she made and is therefore unable to collect the correct amount of tax.

A tax bracket is the level of tax a person is required to pay based on the amount of income she or he makes. A tax writeoff is an amount of money a person can deduct from their income, which may result in she or he paying less tax. A tax return is money given back to a citizen by the government if the citizen overpaid his or her taxes.

Written Response

WRITTEN RESPONSE

How well does the federal political system in Canada govern the country for all Canadians?

Write a response in which you complete the following tasks:

- **Identify** and **explain various positions** regarding how well the federal political system governs Canada.

- **Choose** and **defend a personal point of view** by addressing how the issue illustrates citizenship and identity in Canada.

- **Provide evidence** from what you have learned in your Grade 9 social studies classes to support your ideas.

- **Communicate** your ideas clearly in sentences and paragraphs.

When writing, be sure to take the following steps:

- Remember that the class work you did on the federal political system may have information that could help you write your response.

- Plan and focus your thoughts.

- Support your ideas with evidence.

- Edit your work directly on your writing.

- Budget your time.

PLANNING PAGE

WRITTEN WORK

_____

_____

_____

_____

_____

_____

_____

_____

_____

_____

_____

_____

_____

_____

_____

_____

_____

_____

_____

_____

_____

_____

_____

_____

_____

_____

_____

_____

_____

_____

_____

_____

_____

_____

_____

_____

_____

_____

_____

_____

_____

_____

_____

_____

_____

_____

_____

_____

_____

_____

_____

_____

_____

_____

_____

_____

_____

_____

_____

_____

RUBRIC—WRITING ASSIGNMENT

The following rubric will be used to score your response to the written-response question. It will be helpful for you to review the expectations for each mark to help you focus on specific areas.

There are four categories in the scoring rubric: significance of the issue, personal judgments, supporting evidence, and clarity of communication.

SIGNIFICANCE OF THE ISSUE	
• Understanding of the relevance of the issue to citizenship and identity • Acknowledgement of the viewpoints, perspectives, and values of others	
Excellent E	• The student's understanding of the relevance of the issue is insightful. • The student explores various viewpoints, perspectives, and values in a purposeful manner.
Proficient Pf	• The student's understanding of the relevance of the issue is thoughtful. • The student explores various viewpoints, perspectives, and values in a purposeful manner.
Satisfactory S	• The student's understanding of the relevance of the issue is logical. • The student explores various viewpoints, perspectives, and values in a straightforward manner.
Limited L	• The student's understanding of the relevance of the issue is incomplete. • The student explores various viewpoints, perspectives, and values in a superficial or ambiguous manner.
Poor P	• The student's understanding of the relevance of the issue is minimal. • The student explores various viewpoints, perspectives, and values in an abrupt or uninformed manner.
Insufficient INS	• The marker can discern no evidence of an attempt to address the task presented in the assignment, or the student has written so little that it is not possible to assess the significance of the issue. The response has been awarded an INS for significance of the issue.

	PERSONAL JUDGMENTS

- Choice of position or proposed solution regarding the issue
- Arguments related to the position or ideas regarding the solution presented
- Awareness of the implications of the position or solution advocated

Excellent **E**	• The student's choice of position or proposed solution is perceptive. • The arguments or ideas presented by the student are convincing. • The student demonstrates an astute awareness of the implications of the position or solution advocated.
Proficient **Pf**	• The student's choice of position or proposed solution is sound. • The arguments or ideas presented by the student are considered. • The student demonstrates a sensible awareness of the implications of the position or solution advocated.
Satisfactory **S**	• The student's choice of position or proposed solution is appropriate. • The arguments or ideas presented by the student are predictable. • The student demonstrates an adequate awareness of the implications of the position or solution advocated.
Limited **L**	• The student's choice of position or proposed solution is vague and simplistic. • The arguments or ideas presented by the student are imprecise and lacking. • The student demonstrates a limited awareness of the implications of the position or solution advocated.
Poor **P**	• The student's choice of position or proposed solution is confused and underdeveloped. • The arguments or ideas presented by the student are inaccurate and overgeneralized. • The student demonstrates a questionable awareness of the implications of the position or solution advocated.
Insufficient **INS**	• The marker can discern no evidence of an attempt to address the task presented in the assignment, or the student has written so little that it is not possible to assess personal judgments. The response has been awarded an INS for personal judgments.

SUPPORTING EVIDENCE	
• The student's selection of evidence relative to the issue • The depth, breadth, and accuracy of the evidence provided • The student's integration and application of the evidence to the arguments or ideas presented	
Excellent **E**	• The student has judiciously selected evidence pertinent to the issue. • The evidence provided is precise, comprehensive, and essentially free of factual errors. • The student has skillfully incorporated the evidence chosen in order to reinforce arguments or ideas presented.
Proficient **Pf**	• The student has adeptly selected evidence pertinent to the issue. • The evidence provided is specific, elaborated, and contains few factual errors. • The student has skillfully incorporated the evidence chosen in order to strengthen arguments or ideas presented.
Satisfactory **S**	• The student has generally selected evidence applicable to the issue. • The evidence provided is general and narrow in scope and may contain occasional factual errors. • The student has sufficiently incorporated the evidence chosen in order to reinforce arguments or ideas presented.
Limited **L**	• The student has selected evidence that is insufficient or tenuously related to the issue. • The evidence provided is vague, contradictory, and mere reiteration of information studied or contained in the test, and it may contain frequent factual errors. • The student has skillfully incorporated the evidence chosen in order to reinforce arguments or ideas presented.
Poor **P**	• Evidence selected by the student, if present, is ineffective and tangentially related to the issue. • The evidence, when provided, is scant, obscure, extraneous, and simply copied from the test, and it may contain numerous and glaring factual errors. • The student has haphazardly incorporated what evidence has been chosen, and it does not validate any arguments or ideas presented.
Insufficient **INS**	• The marker can discern no evidence of an attempt to address the task presented in the assignment, or the student has written so little that it is not possible to assess supporting evidence. The response has been awarded an INS for supporting evidence.

	CLARITY OF COMMUNICATION
	• Organization and development of the response • Correct and effective control of mechanics (spelling, punctuation, capitalization) and usage
Excellent **E**	• The response is effectively focused and fluently developed. • The quality of the writing is enhanced because it is essentially free of errors in usage and mechanics.
Proficient **Pf**	• The response is clearly focused and coherently developed. • The quality of the writing is sustained because it contains only minor errors in usage and mechanics.
Satisfactory **S**	• The response is functionally focused and logically developed. • The quality of the writing is acceptable because lapses in usage and mechanics do not detract from overall clarity.
Limited **L**	• The response is weakly focused and uncertainly developed. • The quality of the writing is reduced because it contains frequent errors in usage and mechanics.
Poor **P**	• The response is largely unfocused and unclearly developed. • The quality of the writing is minimized because it contains numerous and glaring errors in usage and mechanics.
Insufficient **INS**	• The marker can discern no evidence of an attempt to address the task presented in the assignment, or the student has written so little that it is not possible to assess clarity of communication. The response has been awarded an INS for clarity of communication.

SOLUTIONS—WRITING ASSIGNMENT

The following example responses to the given writing assignment were written by Grade 9 students. Following each student response is a scoring rubric, demonstrating the mark that each response would receive.

STUDENT SAMPLE RESPONSE 1

Canada's Government

The current federal political system in Canada has changed enormously over the years, and all for the better of out nation. Canada has gone from a ethnocentric, unjust country, to one that all over the world people have grown to respect and ally. We are all very proud of the Democratic system that runs over country and the rights and freedoms given and protected in our charter.

Rights are given to everyone in Canada, no matter if they are long term residence or visiting, nobody is exempt. We supply 3 cultures with "collective rights", that ensure fair treatment towards them in our society. Various legal rights ensure that the justice system is run fairly, in which protecting individual right.

Canada has put forth a "Youth Criminal Justice Act" that is designed to treat young offenders with the fairness they deserve. It was created to give people under 18 a 2nd chance and rehabilitate, so there wouldn't be any second offence. Their main goal is to teach kids that they will be held accountable, and that there is serious consequences. Everyone is involved when crimes are committed, so teaching young offenders this helps them realize the role that they play in society.

We live in a country with Freedoms and rights directed toward everyone. It's in the governments best interest to keep Canada a safe place for all and insure everyone in it is protected. Our government has changed, and is still changing, all for the better of our country and people.

Social Studies Writing Prompt Marking Rubric—Student Sample Response 1

	Significance of the Issue 5 Marks	Personal Judgments 10 Marks	Supporting Evidence 10 Marks	Clarity of Communication 5 Marks
Excellent	E = 5	E = 5 × 2	E = 5 × 2	E = 5
Proficient	Pf = 4	Pf = 4 × 2	Pf = 4 × 2	Pf = 4
Satisfactory	S = 3	S = 3 × 2	S = 3 × 2	S = 3
Limited	L = 2	L = 2 × 2	L = 2 × 2	L = 2
Poor	P = 1	P = 1 × 2	P = 1 × 2	P = 1
Insufficient	INS = 0	INS = 0	INS = 0	INS = 0

Total marks: $\dfrac{26}{30}$

STUDENT SAMPLE RESPONSE 2

> **How well does the Federal Political System govern all of Canada?**
>
> The federal political system governs Canada pretty well. The system is fair and it has a lot of rights and freedoms. Citizenship in Canada is fair to. Everybody has to pay taxes, everybody has the same rights, including immigrants. Canada's economy is stronger because of allowing immigrants into our country. Canada respects people's identity and doesn't try to assimilate them. There are collective and group rights for different cultures. For example: First Nations people, Francophones and Anglophones.
>
> The political system is also fair to people who commit crimes, and children who commit crimes. Nobody in Canada can be prosecuted. Everybody is innocent until proven guilty and children under 12 aren't punished as harshly as adults. The criminal justice system also takes into account disabilities, so to be fair to everyone.
>
> Some of the basic rights people have are the freedom of opinion, and assembly. So you can have your own opinion, express it and challenge authority, Assembly, you can join a political party or create one to try and overthrow the government. Religion and conscience, you can believe in whatever you want and not be judged for it. You can do what you think is right as long as its not illegal. And last, association. You can join whatever party you choose, or group you choose.
>
> Overall, Canadas Federal Political system is a very fair, vary good system. It allows Canada to be a controlled, multi-cultural society that allows the citizens to choose how the country is run. It is free from unfair punishments, such as torture and death, and provides citizens with things like free health care and other services.

Social Studies Writing Prompt Marking Rubric—Student Sample Response 2

	Significance of the Issue 5 Marks	Personal Judgments 10 Marks	Supporting Evidence 10 Marks	Clarity of Communication 5 Marks
Excellent	E = 5	E = 5 × 2	E = 5 × 2	E = 5
Proficient	Pf = 4	Pf = 4 × 2	Pf = 4 × 2	Pf = 4
Satisfactory	S = 3	S = 3 × 2	S = 3 × 2	S = 3
Limited	L = 2	L = 2 × 2	L = 2 × 2	L =2
Poor	P = 1	P = 1 × 2	P = 1 × 2	P = 1
Insufficient	INS = 0	INS = 0	INS = 0	INS = 0

Total Marks: $\dfrac{24}{30}$

STUDENT SAMPLE RESPONSE 3

My opinion on how well the federal political system governs all of Canada is that Canada is doing a good job, but could do better. I know that it is probably very hard to govern a country, but they could be doing a better job. I don't think that they are trying 110% to govern our country. It is very possible for them to improve.

The Youth Criminal Justice Act is one of the good things about how they are governing Canada. I think it is the best punishment for youth if they've done something wrong. They should be held accountable for their actions. If you do some bad, like murdering or stealing, you should be punished. The youth need to know that they can't continue on doing that, and definitely should go through rehab and try to turn their lives around.

It is very fair that Aboriginals, Anglephones and Francophones have collective rights. Immigrants might not think it is fair, but we are the founders of Canada, and should be recognized.

Immigration is another good thing. Canada's population, if we didn't have immigrants wouldn't be enough people to have jobs for the needs that Canadians have. Although, Canada should be a little more strict with who gets in. Sometimes, it seems like everywhere you go, there are immigrants taking over our jobs. The government should have more strict age limits for who gets in. The oldest age should be 50 years old. Canada shouldn't be letting so many immigrants in. It should be about 85% of what they are letting in now.

If people are in prison for murder they should <u>never</u> be let out for good behaviour. That is a terrible decision the government made. Why would you let a murderer out of prison if they haven't been there for their full sentence. It's ridiculous!!! They might just go murder someone else.

Also, it takes too long for some bills to be passed. Although it is good if it takes a long time because they are looking over it and making sure it's good for Canada, there should be a time limit for which a bill is passed. It should take a maximum of 2 years to pass a bill. That is plenty of time.

These are the main reasons why I think the federal political system is doing a good job of governing Canada, but could do better.

Social Studies Writing Prompt Marking Rubric—Student Sample Response 3

	Significance of the Issue 5 Marks	Personal Judgments 10 Marks	Supporting Evidence 10 Marks	Clarity of Communication 5 Marks
Excellent	E = 5	E = 5 × 2	E = 5 × 2	E = 5
Proficient	Pf = 4	Pf = 4 × 2	Pf = 4 × 2	Pf = 4
Satisfactory	S = 3	S = 3 × 2	S = 3 × 2	S = 3
Limited	L = 2	L = 2 × 2	L = 2 × 2	L = 2
Poor	P = 1	P = 1 × 2	P = 1 × 2	P = 1
Insufficient	INS = 0	INS = 0	INS = 0	INS = 0

Total Marks: $\dfrac{22}{30}$

STUDENT SAMPLE RESPONSE 4

In my opinion, I would say Canada is doing an okay job. I think its only okay because the way the government does everything might be helpful for some people but it isn't for most. Like taxes. What I don't understand is the government wants all the homeless people to get jobs and homes. How does the government expect this to happen when taxes keep going up. The government could lower prices of everything. I don't see how hard it could be. To me Canada's governments judgement is clouded. Mine is clear. The only people who can really be happy with the government are the wealthy people.

Trying to understand what everyone in the government is really thinking, confuses me. Like how we deal with criminals. For example a young girl kills her family and goes away for 10 years. An adult would be put away for life for a crime she probably didn't even do. Or say a mother was driving her daughter to school on a stormy day and she crashed and her daughter died. The mother will go away for longer than the young girl who killed her family will. It's unfair. The mother is innocent, and the young girl is a murderer. Sometimes I wish I was a judge just so I could decide on things the fair and responsable way.

I believe that the only the government cares about is money. If all the prices of everything were lowered all familie's would be comfortable wealthy and they could concentrate on things that matter. Like family. Because of taxes and high prices children become separated from their fathers because the best way to make good money is in a camp job. All I say is lower taxes and let family come first. The world will be a better place when money isnt the most important thing.

Social Studies Writing Prompt Marking Rubric—Student Sample Response 4

	Significance of the Issue 5 Marks	Personal Judgments 10 Marks	Supporting Evidence 10 Marks	Clarity of Communication 5 Marks
Excellent	E = 5	E = 5 × 2	E = 5 × 2	E = 5
Proficient	Pf = 4	Pf = 4 × 2	Pf = 4 × 2	Pf = 4
Satisfactory	S = 3	S = 3 × 2	S = 3 × 2	S = 3
Limited	L = 2	L = 2 × 2	L = 2 × 2	L = 2
Poor	P = 1	P = 1 × 2	P = 1 × 2	P = 1
Insufficient	INS = 0	INS = 0	INS = 0	INS = 0

Total Marks: $\dfrac{20}{30}$

STUDENT SAMPLE RESPONSE 5

In my opinion Canada is doing okay but the gov't could inprove. They are doing good with the democracy. In the democracy there can be ragular elections. Also in a democracy there is a choice of parties when there is multiples of them. When the government is accountable it tries to do its best with everything. Thats whats good with democracy.

With the charter there is individual rights. That means everyone has a right. With the charter it is talking about how everyone has the freedom to there opinion. When you believe in something enough and the government doesn't agree, you can say but I have the freedom to my opinion, even look at the charter. Thats what the charter means.

The youth criminal justice act is about when youg people comite a crime. They go there to talk to people about why they did what they did. They also have to talk to a judge to see how long he has to stay there but they don't want to force them to prision. It also wants to treat young people fairly. They like to ensure that youths are held accountable. That why the youth criminal justice act is about.

Social Studies Writing Prompt Marking Rubric—Student Sample Response 5

	Significance of the Issue 5 Marks	Personal Judgments 10 Marks	Supporting Evidence 10 Marks	Clarity of Communication 5 Marks
Excellent	E = 5	E = 5 × 2	E = 5 × 2	E = 5
Proficient	Pf = 4	Pf = 4 × 2	Pf = 4 × 2	Pf = 4
Satisfactory	S = 3	S = 3 × 2	S = 3 × 2	S = 3
Limited	L = 2	L = 2 × 2	L = 2 × 2	L = 2
Poor	P = 1	P = 1 × 2	P = 1 × 2	P = 1
Insufficient	INS = 0	INS = 0	INS = 0	INS = 0

Total Marks: $\dfrac{18}{30}$

Appendices

GLOSSARY

Canada–Quebec Accord	This agreement was signed in 1991. It allows Quebec to choose French-speaking immigrants from around the world to immigrate to Canada, although the federal government officially clears these people for immigration to Canada. In addition, the accord allows Quebec to insist that immigrants send their children to French schools or enroll in French programs.
collectivism	The belief that providing for society as a whole is important.
economic platform	A description of what policies a political party believes are appropriate to maintain and stimulate the country's economy.
executive branch	The branch of the Canadian government that consists of the prime minister, the cabinet, and the public service. Its role is to carry out the laws passed by the legislative branch of the government.
immigration	When people leave their homes to go and live in another country.
Indian Act	A law that was first passed in 1876. Its purpose was to allow the government to administer the rights guaranteed to First Nation's people in the numbered treaties.
individualism	The belief that people should provide for themselves.
judicial branch	The branch of the Canadian government that consists of Canada's courts, including the superior provincial courts, the court of appeal, the Supreme Court of Canada, as well as other federal courts. The judicial branch interprets laws made by the legislative branch to ensure the rights of Canadians are protected.
labour union	A group, usually made up of people in a similar industry, that operates to protect and promote the rights of its workers. Labour unions first started to appear in Canada in the late 1800s as a response to difficult working conditions, long hours, and poor pay.
legislative branch	This branch of the Canadian government is also referred to as Parliament. It consists of the House of Commons, the Senate, and the Governor General. The duty of the legislative branch is to propose, amend, and pass laws in Canada.
lobby groups	Organizations that work to influence government decisions about specific issues.
market economy	An economy in which decisions about production and prices are based on supply and demand with very little or no government intervention. The belief in the importance of competition, private ownership, efficiency, consumer sovereignty, and the pursuit of self-interest as an incentive for hard work are some of the major principles of a market economy.
marketing	The way in which companies convey information about their product to the public and try to influence consumers to buy it.
members of Parliament	People who hold seats in the House of Commons and are elected by the citizens of Canada through a process called "representation by population." Members of Parliament are the representatives of the Canadian citizens.
Métis Settlements General Council	This group works to advocate for the issues of the Métis settlements as a collective and makes some regulations that are binding on all the settlements.

mixed economy	An economy in which private ownership and competition are very important. The government is more heavily involved in a mixed economy than in a market economy.
quality of life	The extent to which a person or group of people is able to achieve well-being. Indicators of quality of life do not only include the extent to which basic needs (such as food, clothing, and shelter) are being met, but other factors as well. Some of these other factors include social or spiritual well-being, such as the ability to speak your own language or practice your chosen religion.
scarcity	An economic condition in which people and society have unlimited wants and needs, but there are limited resources (land, labour, and capital) available.
senators	These people are appointed by the prime minister. Senators represent a variety of political parties and may retain their posts until the age of 75.
values	Demonstrate what a person or society believes to be important.
Youth Criminal Justice Act	This act focuses on the rehabilitation of young criminals but also carries heavier punishment for youths convicted of serious and violent crimes.

CREDITS

Every effort has been made to provide proper acknowledgment of the original sources and to comply with copyright law. However, some attempts to establish original copyright ownership may have been unsuccessful. If copyright ownership can be identified, please notify Castle Rock Research Corporation so that appropriate corrective action can be taken.

Clipart images in this publication are from clipart.com. ©2009 by Jupiterimages Corporation

Practice Test 1

23. Cartoon by Morris. Reprinted by permission of Visual Humour. http://www.businesscartoons.co.uk

26. Cartoon by Morris. Reprinted by permission of Visual Humour. http://www.businesscartoons.co.uk

Practice Test 2

26. Excerpt from "Cod moratorium protested" from http://archives.cbc.ca/economy_business/ natural_resources/clips/1081/. Reprinted with permission of the Canadian Broadcasting Corporation.

44. Cartoon by Morris. Reprinted by permission of Visual Humour. http://www.businesscartoons.co.uk

NOTES

BOOK ORDERING INFORMATION
ELEMENTARY and JUNIOR HIGH TITLES

Castle Rock Research offers the following resources to support Alberta students. You can order any of these materials online at:

www.castlerockresearch.com/store

SOLARO - Online Learning		The KEY	SNAP	Prob Solved	Class Notes
$29.95 ea.*		$29.95 ea.*	$29.95 ea.*	$19.95 ea.*	$19.95 ea.*
English Language Arts 9	English Language Arts 6	English Language Arts 9	Science 9	Science 9	Science 9
English Language Arts 8	English Language Arts 5	English Language Arts 6	Mathematics 9	Mathematics 9	Mathematics 9
English Language Arts 7	English Language Arts 4	English Language Arts 3	Mathematics 8	Mathematics 8	Mathematics 8
Mathematics 9	English Language Arts 3	Mathematics 9	Mathematics 7	Mathematics 7	Mathematics 7
Mathematics 8	Mathematics 6	Mathematics 8	Mathematics 6		
Mathematics 7	Mathematics 5	Mathematics 7	Mathematics 5		
Science 9	Mathematics 4	Mathematics 6	Mathematics 4		
Science 8	Mathematics 3	Mathematics 4	Mathematics 3		
Science 7	Science 6	Mathematics 3			
Social Studies 9	Science 5	Science 9			
Social Studies 6	Science 4	Science 6			
	Science 3	Social Studies 9			
		Social Studies 6			

Prices do not include taxes or shipping.

Study online using **SOLARO,** with access to multiple courses available by either a monthly or an annual subscription.

The KEY Study Guide is specifically designed to assist students in preparing for unit tests, final exams, and provincial examinations.

The **Student Notes and Problems (SNAP) Workbook** contains complete explanations of curriculum concepts, examples, and exercise questions.

The **Problem Solved** contains exercise questions and complete solutions.

The **Class Notes** contains complete explanations of curriculum concepts.

If you would like to order Castle Rock resources for your school, please visit our school ordering page:
www.castlerockresearch.com/school-orders/